BIG PICTURE PARTNERING

BIG PICTURE
Partnering

16 weeks to a rock-solid relationship

DR. JAN HOISTAD

Twofold Publications

Minneapolis, Minnesota

Twofold Publications, P.O. Box 50204, Minneapolis, Minnesota 55405

1-888-231-2993, info@twofoldpublications.com

Available through your favorite wholesaler or Midpoint Trade Books at 913-831-2233

Printed in the United States of America

08 07 06 05 04   5 4 3 2 1

Book design by Dorie McClelland, Spring Book Design

Cover design by Deb Miner

Cover photo by Ann Marsden

Library of Congress Control Number: 2003195000

Publisher's Cataloging-in-Publication
(Provided by Quality Books, Inc.)

Hoistad, Jan.
    Big picture partnering : 16 weeks to a rock-solid relationship / Jan Hoistad.
    p.cm.
    ISBN 0-9745351-8-4

    1. Man-woman relationships. 2. Couples--Life skills guides. 3. Interpersonal relations. I. Title.

HQ801.H65 2004   306.7
                QBI33-1666

To my parents and grandparents,
from whom I learned my first lesson about partnering:
that it takes commitment, tenacity, creativity,
and an enormous amount of love.

CONTENTS

PART II.   CREATING A LIFE TOGETHER

. . . .

The Secret of Lasting Love

Creating your Big Picture adventure together

If you were asked to describe the big picture of your relationship with your spouse or partner, what would happen inside of you?

- Your heart would start to flutter with the excitement of your newfound love, your new dreams, and your new hopes together.

- You'd pause and feel the warmth you have for your partner—a warmth that often gets buried under piles of laundry or bills, but quickly surfaces again when given the opportunity.

- You'd yearn for some time and freedom to be alone with your partner—away from the kids and your careers and the endless responsibilities that have taken over much of your lives.

- You'd remember the dreams the two of you have talked about accomplishing together for so long, but have never been able to attain.

- You'd remember the way you felt long ago, when you and your partner first fell in love—and you'd wonder how so many of those feelings had disappeared over the years.

- You'd wonder, now that the kids are finally grown up or you're nearing retirement, if the two of you can renew the passion and commitment you felt for each other so many years ago.

- You'd feel both frightened and hopeful—hopeful because, after a string of poor choices, you've finally committed yourself to some-one wonderful, but frightened that you may have somehow made the same mistakes all over again.

If any of these feelings resonates inside you, welcome. You've come to the right place—a place that helps couples create lives of commitment, support, adventure, and joy.

This book is about Big Picture partnering—being together with your partner in a way that is consistently nourishing, affirming, and downright wonderful. It also means creating a partnership that stays rock-solid, because both of you are getting what you most want in your lives, and consistently creating and living your dreams together.

Big Picture partnering isn't just a skill or technique. It's a whole way of being in a partnership—and of being together in the world.

Big Picture partnering isn't therapy, either. It's not about fixing what's supposedly wrong with either of you, or with your relationship. Nor is Big Picture partnering just a way to reduce conflict or create harmony. Though these will probably happen, this book asks you to think far bigger.

Big Picture partnering is for adults who want to live the life of their dreams together–a life full of bounty, creativity, and possibility. It's for people who want to fulfill their life's mission as a couple. It's for people who sense that their partnership can be more than a convenience or a pleasure or a beneficial exchange—it can make their lives sing with richness and meaning and delight.

This book will lead you through a 16-week process that will teach you and your partner the 10 Essentials of successful partnering, then help you to clarify your values, accomplish goals together, dream together, and then—day by day and year by year—turn those dreams into reality. Along the way it will show both of you how to synchronize yourselves in a true partnership—without giving away any of your essential individuality or autonomy.

Each chapter will teach you and your partner new and valuable skills and concepts; each will provide both of you with opportunities for growth, communication, and practicing Big Picture partnering skills.

Typically, couples move through one chapter a week, which means that in 16 weeks—less than four short months—they build all the skills they need to maintain a Big Picture partnership for a lifetime. But the 16-week timeline is not mandatory. Many couples move more slowly or more quickly through the chapters, adapting them to suit their own schedules and needs.

One thing about Big Picture partnering that doesn't matter is your age. Big Picture partnering can work for adults of any age, from teenagers to couples well into retirement. It doesn't matter what gender you are, what religion you do or don't practice, or whether you and your partner are married. All you need is an honest and earnest commitment to one another, and a desire to live a full, delicious, joyous life together.

How do I know that Big Picture partnering works? I know it because I've been training couples in it for over 15 years, both in workshops on the subject and in counseling sessions. Time after time, year after year, I've watched couples use Big Picture partnering to blossom together, to deepen their commitment to one another, and to build the lives they most want to lead together.

As a psychologist, I've worked with couples, individuals, and organizations since 1979, and regularly lead workshops on Big Picture partnering at sites in the United States and Canada. Many of the people who attend these workshops, and who get the most out of them, are unconventional couples leading mainstream lives. They are couples with a visionary approach to life—people who aren't satisfied with the traditional, solve-my-problems approach to every day and the world. (If you want to know more about what I do, how I work, and what workshops are scheduled for the near future, visit my website at www.bigpicturepartnering.com.)

This book offers you both an opportunity and a challenge. Using it, you and your partner can begin to envision—and then create—your own ideal life together, a life of profound fulfillment, purpose, and mutual support. Or, you can put down this book and your partnership will likely continue to be exactly the way it is right now. It's your call.

Look back at the beginning of this introduction once again. If any of the voices on that first page sounds like yours—or if you yearn for a partnership that can nourish, support, and delight you for a lifetime—keep reading. You can look forward to a partnership that can enrich, empower, and enliven you both for a lifetime.

PART I

Envisioning Together

· ·

Discovering Your Partnering Styles

What comes naturally
and how you'd like it to be

As we look at different couples, we recognize different ways of being in relationships. The more conscious we become about different relationship styles and what they offer, the more choices we have in building a relationship that suits our particular needs.

This week we're going to consider four styles of relating:

• Traditional style
• Merged style
• Roommate style
• Big Picture partnering style

Each style is distinguished by how the two people make decisions and connect with one another.

The four styles will form a backdrop from which you can consciously choose how you want to build your most intimate relationship.

THE TRADITIONAL STYLE

The first way of relating is the one most likely modeled by your grandparents or parents: the Traditional style. The Traditional style has been a given in marriage for many generations and across many cultures. You may recognize aspects of this style in your own relationship.

Simply illustrated, the Traditional style might look like this.

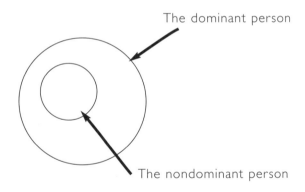

The dominant person

The nondominant person

In the Traditional style of relationship,
one person has more power, especially in decision making.

The Traditional style implies that one person has more power than the other. This does not necessarily mean that the dominant partner misuses or abuses their power. What it does mean is that one person in the couple is dominant, particularly when it comes to making ultimate decisions for the pair. The taking on of this dominant role by one person —male or female—may occur because that person is more forceful or opinionated, or because their partner is more passive and malleable. Or, as was often the case in our grandparents' day, the dominant decision-making role is automatically given to the man, simply because tradition dictates that's how it should be. In some circumstances, this clarifies roles and saves time.

When it is a consciously-chosen approach to relating, the Traditional style can be a viable model. Even today, many couples experience highly successful traditional relationships. Many who choose this style will defend it by pointing out that it results in the successful circumventing of potential power struggles and conflicts. Some even feel it is a God-given preference. The Traditional style can spell out roles and tasks very clearly when there are young children to raise or when one person has the main bread-winning function and is on a career path that requires intense involvement.

For example, Al is a high-level vice president in a midwestern company. He comes from a culture of traditional family values. He and Sharon are in their thirties, with three children under the age of nine. Sharon is a stay-at-home mom and a stand-by-your-man kind of woman. She never questions Al's work choices, including their frequent job-related moves. She and the kids have had a hard time making long-term friendships. She hopes they stay in this town until the kids have grown, but that decision will be left to Al. Sharon is proud to be at Al's side at church and at community and social events. They are both pleased with her role as Al's wife, and with her abilities as a homemaker. She has dinner on the table at seven, shortly after Al arrives home from the office. If they have plans to go out for the evening, Sharon will have made arrangements for the sitter.

Al spends time with the children after dinner until Sharon takes over and gets them ready for bed.

The opportunity for connection and intimacy-building in the Traditional style is dependent upon the choices, needs, and desire of the person with the most power. When that person, usually the husband, feels that time with their partner is important and valuable, then talking, affection, and sex may occur on a regular and mutually-fulfilling basis.

Amanda talks about growing up and watching her aunt and uncle interact.

> *My Aunt Katherine was a stay-at-home mom who raised four children while Uncle Jim worked on the road in construction. Although Uncle Jim had the last word, he always supported my aunt's mothering and decisions. He worked hard all day and she treated him like a king when he came home at night. He was involved with his family in the evenings. Katherine was sassy and flirty, playful and fun as a mother and as a wife. Jim showed his playfully exuberant affection for her in front of the kids, and often included them in the affection as well. When they could afford it, they took the time to be alone with each other, letting Grandma come to stay with the kids.*

If, however, the dominant person is out of touch with the other person's needs, or just doesn't think those needs are important, then connection and intimacy may not be present.

For example, Monica and Evan married in their late teens. Monica came from a broken home, where she parented her younger siblings and protected them as best she could from their alcoholic mother and the dysfunctional behavior of both parents. Soon after they married, Monica and Evan discovered they were pregnant. Monica quit her job and became a stay-at-home mom. She ran a smooth household, and

Evan provided a healthy income. Monica has since developed skills doing bookkeeping for small independent contractors; however, she feels she could more fully develop this business if Evan were more supportive of her. Now in her mid-thirties, with two teenage daughters, Monica feels that Evan has all the power in the relationship. Evan earns most of the income and handles the upkeep of their cars and property. Monica handles child rearing, schedules, and their social calendar. She wants the two of them to socialize more with friends. He wants to stay home in the evenings. He seems unaware of her needs for time, attention, affection, and sex, even though she says she asks him for these things. She has to get angry with him in order for him to treat her needs as valid. As you can see, in this Traditional household, both parties are not always satisfied.

Let's summarize the means of decision making, the manner of connecting, and the potential for intimacy building in the Traditional style of relating.

> IN THE TRADITIONAL STYLE OF RELATING:
> One member of the pair is dominant and makes the ultimate decision for both partners. The agreement to adhere to this style may be spoken or unspoken—or there may be no conscious agreement by both partners.

In such a relationship, the person with the most power determines the kind, quality, and amount of connection and whether that connection is given or received. Thus, the potential for intimacy-building is dependent upon the capacity for intimacy of the person who makes the decisions. Yet, only two whole individuals can achieve true intimacy.

THE MERGED STYLE

In the Merged style of relating, individuals in a couple have no personal boundaries. They are what we call codependent, interdependent, and almost interchangeable in their thoughts, feelings, interests, and desires. This is because they have failed to develop whole separate selves or identities. As the diagram below shows, they share the same psychological, mental, and emotional space.

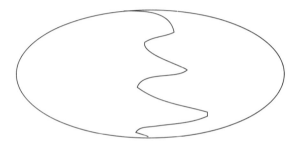

In the Merged style of relating,
two people are halves of a whole—
codependent, interdependent, and interchangeable
in thoughts, feelings, interests, and desires.

Decision making for the Merged couple appears seamless. They go along with one another, because they seldom do or decide anything that would be surprising or unusual. Typically, they stick to prescribed and expected choices, decisions, and responses, and they know exactly what to expect from one another. Often, the person who is the least passive at that moment voices a preference and the partner just goes along.

When you're around such couples, you might notice that they may finish one another's thoughts, not just sentences, and have such a uniform point of view that they seem to have little individuality. Their closeness may appear as intimacy, while their responses or thoughts may seem rote, rigid, and routine. They are often inseparable, sometimes in an almost charming way, as in very old couples who have been together for fifty or sixty years. However, when one partner is away, the other one doesn't know what to do, or even think, because they are truly lost without their other half. We have also heard stories and statistics about older people who die within a short time of their partner's death, unable to tolerate being alone.

Some couples evolve into this Merged relationship if they are together for a long time and fail to develop individual interests or receive support for individual growth. Dorothy and Bill are a case in point. They met in their early twenties, lived within the same few blocks in pre-World War II New York City, and shared the same culture. Both were the children of Italian immigrants. Bill's grandfather owned a small neighborhood grocery store, and when his grandfather unexpectedly passed away, Bill dropped out of high school to run the store. When Dorothy and Bill married, they moved into the living space above the store. Having cheerful dispositions, they never argued and easily agreed upon the decisions that faced them daily.

For the next fifty-plus years, Bill and Dorothy operated the store, and, except for the short times Dorothy spent in the hospital having their three children, they were together for almost twenty-four hours a day.

When they reached their early seventies, they allowed one of their daughters to purchase the store, which she converted into a coffee shop. Bill and Dorothy continued to live above the shop, spending all their time together, until Bill passed away from a heart attack.

After his death, Dorothy was extremely despondent. She told her daughter that she couldn't live without Bill. This proved to be true. Dorothy's despondency was detrimental to her health. Within a month of Bill's passing, Dorothy developed pneumonia, from which she had no will to recover. She passed away in a matter of days.

Younger couples, too, can become merged—especially teenage brides and grooms, who wed before their individual personalities are fully formed. Chet and Sue first met in their ninth-grade science class as lab partners. Each of them describes their meeting as love at first sight. They were inseparable throughout high school. They signed up for the same classes and attended the same after-school activities. When Chet made the football team, Sue became a cheerleader. Because they spent the majority of their free time together, neither one of them developed close friendships outside their relationship. Chet was able to develop skills as a carpenter while working at his father's construction company during summer breaks. Sue was able to work in the company's small office. They married the summer after they graduated high school, and in the next four years had two children. Their lives were fairly uneventful. They both followed the same daily routines, and even went to the same location for their yearly vacation. They spent ten years in this fashion, and then, about two months ago, a change occurred.

The small construction firm where Chet is employed expanded to include locations in several surrounding states. As lead carpenter, Chet is now required to oversee a number of these projects. He spends many weekdays at motels near his worksite and comes home on the weekends. As a result, Chet and Sue are both spending time on their own for the first time since they met. Sue feels that she has nothing to do when away from Chet. She has made no significant friendships and has developed no personal interests of her own. She says that she feels like this would be disloyal to Chet. Now Sue finds herself asking, "Is this all there is?" She is growing dissatisfied with what she calls "the same day over and over again," but she is unable to define what she would like to change. She feels that she is living for the weekends, when Chet is home.

Although Chet and Sue feel it is romantic to be so intertwined—believing they are "two against the world"—Sue is finding it difficult to develop her own interests while Chet is away during the week. Chet, on the other hand, is able to function separately from Sue, but he doesn't enjoy his time with the guys on the site or make friends easily. He's not used to socializing without Sue and is uncomfortable on his own. He relies on his weekend time with Sue to recharge his batteries, and this is putting great stress on their marriage.

Like Chet and Sue, Merged couples have not fully developed their individual personalities—or their individual interests, activities, thoughts, or feelings. Thus, they are limited to a narrow range of behaviors and interactions. They have developed no skills to identify their individual feelings, wants, and needs. When they are on their own they are not able to define and verbalize their dissatisfaction and loneliness. When they step outside of their merged bounds, they are often "lost." Chet feels lost away from Sue and cannot connect to his coworkers. Sue has only a limited ability to expand her activities and continues to feel unfulfilled on her own during the week.

When they're alone, the individuals in a Merged couple feel vulnerable. They only feel whole and safe when they are together.

Decision making for the Merged couple is made by adhering to the cultural stereotypes of our society; that is, by doing what may be typically expected of a husband or wife or partner without giving it much thought. In addition, without an awareness of individual needs and feelings, the Merged couple is not able to understand and share true intimacy, which requires the coming together of two whole, mature selves.

IN THE MERGED STYLE:
Decisions are made by adhering to the cultural stereotypes of our society, so it will appear as if the couple is always in agreement, but the agreements are within a narrow range of what is acceptable and expected. In the Merged relationship, the two people are fused rather than separate individuals intimately connecting or interacting. This limits the potential for true intimacy.

THE ROOMMATE STYLE

The third model of relating applies not only to actual roommates and friends, but to long-term couples as well. When applied to couples in a long-term romantic relationship, the Roommate style describes two people of equal power and competency in the world who share a home and other significant aspects of their lives. In addition to living together, they typically have sex, share some friends, and may even have a child. A major defining characteristic of the Roommate style is that individuals in the couple each make decisions unilaterally.

A Roommate style relationship might be diagrammed as on the next page.

For instance, a woman may come home one evening and tell her partner she's going out with her friends on Friday night (implying that he has to watch the kids, get a sitter, or fend for himself). A man might not feel it necessary to consult his partner when he chooses to quit or change his job. Either their money is totally separate, or it is implied that she'll just have to make a financial adjustment for a time.

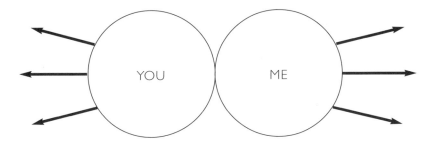

In The Roommate style of relating, individuals are relatively equal in strength and power. they may share many things, but they make decisions unilaterally; connection happens at random.

Let's look at the relationship of Rahlah and Jeremy. They met through mutual friends and have been married for four years. Jeremy is an architect, and, except for a serious college romance, he had been fully engaged in his career . . . until he met Rahlah. Rahlah, like Jeremy, is in her early thirties. She started a small dot-com company, through which she sells handmade specialty soaps. Rahlah has been making and selling soap successfully for over ten years. Jeremy was attracted and impressed by what he calls her "low maintenance" way of operating.

When Jeremy was offered a position with a prestigious firm on the East Coast, he was thrilled and accepted the offer without talking it over with his wife. Rahlah was delighted for him, and she was not in the least disturbed that her husband had not consulted her before making the decision to move several states away. Rahlah was confident that her business would do well "no matter where we live," and she enjoys that her husband is "as independent as I am." They have chosen to put off having children for now, and Rahlah has expressed concern that some adjustments in their lifestyles might be necessary when they have kids:

I'm afraid we are both so focused on ourselves that we won't know how to work together if we have kids. I'll end up having to take care of them, unless Jeremy wants to in his off time.

Neither Rahlah nor Jeremy is dissatisfied with the amount of connection and intimacy they currently have because they are both so involved with their work lives. When they do come together it is satisfying. Rahlah, however, is anticipating that if they have children she may desire more participation from Jeremy, as well as more connection and intimacy. If they do have children, the Roommate style of relating may no longer be satisfying.

Like Jeremy and Rahlah, partners in the Roommate style of relating come and go pretty much at will. This is done with the expectation that the other person, and maybe even the children, will make necessary adjustments without any discussion. Sometimes this works and people are happy with the outcome, but when it doesn't work, at least one person will be left unhappy and, sometimes, unaware of what is wrong.

What distinguishes these relationships is the independent activity of each person and their ability to make solo decisions even when such decisions affect both partners—and, perhaps, an entire family. In this model, the one partner's needs may or may not be taken into consideration, and their concerns may or may not be addressed. Decision making is one-sided, even when the deciding partner has the best of intentions and feels that they are accommodating their partner's unspoken desires.

David and Margie provide another example of the Roommate decision-making process. A bright, energetic, thirty-something couple, they have been together for about a year. He is a self-made, successful entrepreneur; she is well educated in business and finance. He is suburban/rural; she is city-raised. Together they are working to create a unique and thriving business in the suburb of a large metropolitan area. Having recently moved into David's home, they are struggling to work out a mutual approach to relating. (Such struggles are common at this stage in a relationship.)

David is a well-intentioned man who loves his down-to-earth but worldly and savvy Margie very much. He is committed to learning how to do this relationship differently, having previously suffered through a divorce. He is, however, clearly vacillating in his approach to decision making. On the one hand, he talks over every business decision with Margie; on the other hand, he made reservations for their honeymoon without finalizing the specific date of the wedding or discussing the final location of the honeymoon with her.

Another defining characteristic of the Roommate style is that opportunities for connection occur only randomly, since partners tend to function independently. This means there might be a steady connection at times, but only an intermittent connection at others. Feeling connected cannot be counted on because one partner may make other plans or find something more important to attend to at any given time.

While some couples consciously choose the Roommate style, many don't actually set out to become roommates. Modern couples often fall into this style of relating by default rather than choice. Most people are not educated in how to build and sustain a truly intimate partnership. Perhaps they saw their parents relating in this way. Or the Roommate style may have unconsciously developed as a way to avoid closeness—the result of previous disappointments and the inability to trust. Some of my clients even point out that the Roommate style can be the result of having to be strong and independent in their jobs and careers, and never having learned another way of interacting in close relationships.

Some couples have relative success in the Roommate style when life is going fairly smoothly. I have also heard of couples being satisfied with this model when one or both have easy going, non-goal-oriented, laid-back personalities. Typically this relaxed attitude is accompanied by knowledge that "my partner probably wouldn't change even if I asked them." Often, one or both individuals are conflict-avoidant.

On the other hand, because this way of relating is typically not consciously chosen, and because partners cannot always count on connecting with each other, the Roommate style often leads to misunderstanding and dissatisfaction for one or both people.

IN THE ROOMMATE STYLE:
Decision making is unilateral. Each person makes decisions individually, without necessarily consulting the other. The expectation is that each person will adjust to the decisions made uni-laterally by the other.

Connection happens at random. It may happen frequently, intermittently, or very little, depend-ing on each person's choices at any given time. While there may be two whole individuals in the Roommate relationship, this style results in ten-uous opportunity for intimacy-building, at best.

THE BIG PICTURE PARTNERING STYLE

The fourth way of relating is the Big Picture partnering style. When you and your partner relate in this way, you mutually create three worlds, which are encompassed in a larger partnering universe.

In the following diagrams, the circle on the left symbolizes *your world:* comprises all your individual uniqueness, friends, work, finances, activities, and so on. The circle on the right is *your partner's world:* comprises all the aspects of your partner's life. The center circle encompasses the mutually-chosen and mutually-created aspects of your life as a couple, which only you two unique human beings can build together.

You will notice in the diagram that there is a table just outside of the *our world* circle. This symbolizes the Big Picture approach to communication and to reaching agreement together. In effect, each partner brings their thoughts, concerns, needs, wants, and desires to the table, where they are freely discussed until the two of you arrive at a mutual decision regarding how you want to act on this aspect of your partnering life together.

Here is an example of how this works. Milo and Irina have been married thirteen years and have three children. Whenever Milo has a big decision to make about his work life, he brings it home and talks it over with Irina before committing to any major changes. He and Irina try to make all such major decisions together. "It may take us a little longer to talk everything over," he says, "but in the long run we are both happier. We are a family, and my job is, in many ways, 'our job.' Irina's happiness and the stability of our three kids is important to me. I value her opinion and really want her support in everything I do. So we make these kinds of decisions together."

Unlike the other models of relating previously described, in the Big Picture partnering style, one world does not take away from another.

**In the Big Picture Partnering Universe
your relationship is:**

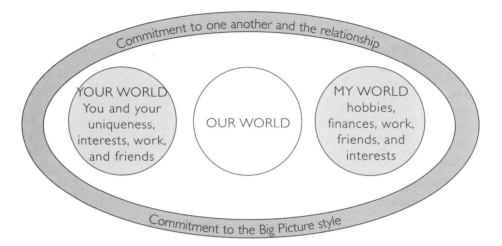

Supported and strengthened by your commitments

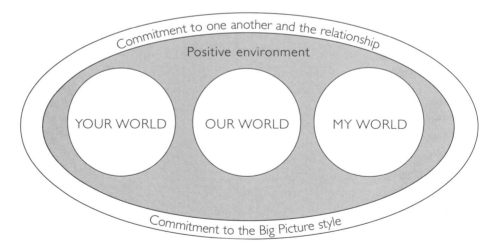

Nurtured by positive feelings, regular talking and listening,
and Essentials that build trust and connection

In Big Picture partnering:

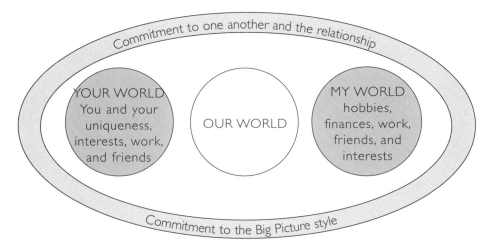

Both of you bring your uniqueness, individual lives,
needs, desires, and dreams to the relationship

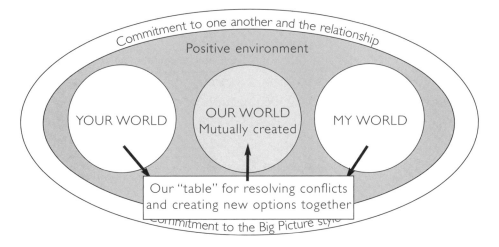

You come together to create your unique and mutually satisfying *our world*;
nothing goes into *our world* until it has been agreed upon by the two of you.

Irina describes other aspects of their lives that she and Milo freely decide on—together, in the case of major decisions, and separately, in the case of minor ones.

I feel secure in knowing that we make all the major decisions together. We emigrated from Russia just after we were married, and I was pregnant. At the time we needed to be very connected—on everything—just to survive in this new country. We really learned how to work together. Over time, as we have become acclimated and at home here, we each have lots of separate activities, not only with the kids, but we are very social and have friends individually and couple friends together. Now that our six-year-old is in school, I have a part-time job, and this is my spending money separate from the family account. Milo takes his own allowance for his activities. I like to take pottery classes, and he is studying how to tutor other immigrants coming into the country. Along with our active kids, it makes for an exciting mix in our marriage!

In Big Picture partnering, having two strong individual worlds and an *our world* together is important. When you follow the 10 Essentials of Big Picture partnering on the next page which you will learn during the coming weeks, all three worlds coexist harmoniously. Using this approach, you will practice developing and balancing all three worlds in order to enjoy a richer and more rewarding relationship.

These 10 Essentials are designed to help you support, nurture, protect, and express your relationship. While I encourage couples to incorporate other useful ideas for building and maintaining a wonderful partnership, if you do nothing else, follow these 10 Essentials and your relationship will become rock solid. They work.

In the coming weeks, you will have the opportunity to practice and experience the 10 Essentials and discover your own unique values, needs, dreams, and goals.

THE 10 ESSENTIALS
OF BIG PICTURE PARTNERING

1 Create and maintain positive feelings between you.

2 Talk together regularly, and take turns listening.

3 Regularly renew your commitment to one another—and to your relationship.

4 Stay committed to the Big Picture partnering style.

5 Make win/win decisions together.

6 Pull your weight in the partnership, no matter what your partner is doing.

7 Make and keep clear agreements with one another.

8 Remind yourselves that partnering is a joint effort.

9 Address any problem in your relationship together—whether it's *yours, mine,* or *ours.*

10 Resolve conflicts and create new options together through dialogue and imagination.

You and your partner will practice these 10 Essentials in a step-by-step fashion as you are guided in both individual and joint exercises. Some exercises will ask you to step back and look at the big picture of your relationship—what you value, desire, and envision. Others will require that you zoom in and focus on applying your big picture considerations and desires to the daily details of life—how you manage everything from household chores and schedules to finances, sexuality, and minor disagreements. Each week's learning will build on the previous week's lessons until you gradually incorporate all 10 Essentials of the Big Picture partnering style into your daily, weekly, and monthly routines. Each week, as you incorporate these guidelines and tools, you will build together a rock-solid foundation for a relationship that rocks.

BIG PICTURE PARTNERING MEANS DECIDING AND CREATING TOGETHER

When you choose the Big Picture style, the way in which you and your partner make decisions is quite different from that of the other three styles. In the Traditional style, one person usually makes the decisions for both people. In the Merged style, decisions are based on cultural stereotypes and are thus limited in their scope. And in the Roommate style, each partner often makes decisions independently of the other. In the Big Picture, *our world* decisions—those that involve both people—are made together. *Your world* and *my world* decisions are made individually, but are supported by each partner.

IN BIG PICTURE PARTNERING:
any issue can be brought to the table for
discussion; however, nothing goes into the

our world circle until it is fully agreed upon by both individuals. Couples who do Big Picture partnering use the 10 Essentials for communicating and interacting. These 10 Essentials promote mutual, creative decision making.

Big Picture decision making is not necessarily about compromise. Nor is it about neglecting your own needs in order to attend only to those of your partner. Big Picture partnering isn't about giving in or settling. Rather, it challenges both partners to become creative, to recognize or invent new options together. This approach helps you master the fine art of blending each of your needs into something totally new and unique—an *our world* that satisfies both of you.

When two people make a decision to work as Big Picture partners, nothing goes into the partnership circle until it has been mutually agreed upon.

One-time decisions—about what to have for dinner, which movie to go to, or whether to stay home on Friday night—are easy. But sometimes, Big Picture partnering means that partners will discuss and mull things over for a number of weeks. For instance, shortly after Marybeth and Ron got married, they began to pursue the topic of buying a house. It was a loaded topic because Marybeth wanted to live in the city and Ron had always wanted a home on a lake. At the time, they found it hard to imagine how this might be resolved to the satisfaction of both. Agreeing to practice their partnering skills, they spent much time talking, looking, doing research, and investigating their alternating openness and resistance to one another's desire. They took turns looking by lakes and looking in the city. Then they found a little dream home in an unexpected place—halfway between country and city.

The Big Picture partnering skills—the 10 Essentials—helped them put a new home into their *our world* circle within eight months. They have had no regrets. Not long ago, Marybeth called to say,

> *I am still surprised at how Ron and I were able to come together on a decision when we initially appeared to be so far apart in what we wanted. Our choice of a little house near one of the inner suburban lakes has pleased both of us.*

Since purchasing the home nine years ago, Marybeth and Ron have partnered on many other decisions. They have remodeled and expanded their little house; they landscaped the yard; Ron moved his offices out of the house; and they are raising three boys and a family dog—all in that home.

During the next fifteen weeks I will walk you through the steps of Big Picture partnering so you, too, can learn to negotiate and create the outcomes the two of you most desire. This process will sometimes lead—or even force—you to come up with entirely new and unexpected options. The development of your mutual ingenuity is a cocreative undertaking. As you become good at it, not only will you find yourselves discovering mutually agreeable solutions to previously unresolvable problems, you'll also enjoy more fun and spontaneity. As you apply the essential elements of Big Picture partnering to such conflicts, you'll discover, to your delight, that the two of you have grown closer—and happier—in the process. And more energy will be freed up for enjoying your life together.

BIG PICTURE PARTNERING MEANS CONNECTING TO YOUR PARTNER IN A NEW WAY

How does Big Picture partnering allow for a new kind of connection? By enhancing and drawing on one another's individuality—a primary requirement for true connection and intimacy. Big Picture relationships nurture intimacy, unlike Traditional relationships, in which one person has relinquished their power and some of their individuality, or Merged relationships, in which both individuals have given up their uniqueness by fusing together, or Roommate relationships, in which partners may or may not connect depending on their independent decisions.

As you use the Big Picture approach in the coming weeks, you will clearly experience the many and consistent opportunities for connection which are built into partnering. In fact, you cannot truly engage in Big Picture partnering unless you connect often and consistently. At first, you will be guided to communicate in small increments and to apply these communications to important daily basics. Gradually you will expand these skills as you apply them not only to deeper issues that may be more difficult to resolve, but also to creating your future dreams together.

Communicating and interacting, in and of themselves, do not ensure that you will feel emotionally, mentally, or spiritually connected all the time. That is unrealistic. However, the Big Picture partnering will help you create more opportunities for meaningful connection, which is the stepping-stone to intimacy.

The 10 Essentials of Big Picture partnering help strengthen communication and interaction between partners. Using this approach, couples connect frequently and consistently. They connect about everyday details as well as about their future big picture. With their focus on becoming more creative and fulfilling both individual and mutual needs together, they have greater opportunities for experiencing intimacy.

BIG PICTURE PARTNERING MEANS BALANCING INDIVIDUALITY AND MUTUALITY

Couples who do Big Picture partnering bring to their relationships two distinct and unique individual selves who consciously choose to be connected. They desire to support one another's strong sense of individuality while also promoting the mutual decisions of the *our world* they create.

Each member of such a couple brings to their relationship the totality of their uniqueness—their self-expression, wants, desires, talents, and dreams—because they enjoy and relish the richness of their individual lives. At the same time, they passionately want to create with their partner a long-lasting relationship, a joint creation that will add to what they already have individually. The resulting relationship thus becomes a mutual creation made of the inspiration, imagination, personal histories, experiences, gifts, and resources of the two partners. Together they create a feast of a relationship.

Big Picture partnering involves two whole individuals, complete with unique lives, histories, interests, and dreams, working individually to become fully self-expressive, and working mutually to create their long-term relationship.

Big Picture partnering results in two partners who continuously and easily meet both individual and *our world* needs, and who approach interaction and communication as cocreative acts.

BIG PICTURE PARTNERING MEANS REAPING THE BENEFITS OF MUTUAL CREATIVITY

Let me tell you about Harvey and Lenore. In their early fifties, each was on their second marriage. They had been together for seven years when I met them. "We are at a wonderful time of our lives and want to do something totally different," Harvey explained. "We just don't know what that is. All we know is we want to live in a warmer climate as we get older, and we want to do something more fun!" Lenore especially wanted to live in a smaller and more eco-friendly community. Neither of them was sure how to make these parts of their dream into a whole. "We'll probably make a change in five or six years," Harvey told me, not knowing the power of the Big Picture.

Harvey had been a successful corporate executive for many years, and he had a love of mountain climbing, which he seldom had time to do. He wanted to try something entrepreneurial and thought one avenue might be to offer training and consulting to companies in how to go through difficult changes. Or maybe he could write. Or . . . he really wasn't sure. Lenore worked as an office manager for a local arts organization and wanted to keep doing something in the arts. She also wanted to explore her writing talents.

As they had discussions about their values and dreams, Harvey and Lenore eagerly began using the 10 Essentials. They started to experiment with different job ideas and traveled to explore different parts of the country where they might live. After five months, they arrived at a totally unexpected plan, all due to their brainstorming, experimenting, and exploring. Here's how Harvey explained the process:

> *We thought we would explore the temperate parts of the West Coast and ended up spending the last four weeks in Bend, Oregon. We met the nicest people, it's beautiful, and I've decided it's the perfect place to start a mountain climbing and hiking business for anyone—maybe even corporate execs, with treks to Mt. Hood and the surrounding area.*

Harvey was jazzed. It was entrepreneurial, and different from his corporate job, yet it included knowledge of what execs might need. He had met some folks doing similar things in Bend, and they had invited him to explore building this aspect of their sporting company. Lenore had fallen in love with the high desert climate and made friends with a local community organization that worked to protect the environment. She was enthusiastic about the area and her new job prospects:

> *They need someone to help them organize and write for them. I'm good at both, and it would be about twenty-five hours a week so I could also work on my novel.*

Within nine months, Harvey and Lenore were excitedly closing on the sale of their home in Minneapolis and moving to Oregon. They still write or call once in awhile. In our last conversation, Lenore told me:

> *I can't tell you how delighted we continue to be with the changes we made eleven years ago. To think that we could still be stuck in our old rut—but you got us working together and the changes happened so quickly. We are still both surprised.*

BIG PICTURE PARTNERING MEANS APPLYING CREATIVITY TO DAILY DETAILS

Why is it that we rarely manage to resolve with our partner those constant arguments about the little things in life? We spend so much energy hassling over whose turn it is to do the dishes, why the kids aren't finishing their breakfast, or which set of in-laws to invite for the holidays.

Big Picture partnering will provide you with a set of tools to apply to such daily problems, so that you can clarify and come to mutual agreements about them. For each couple, the list of issues that cause frequent arguments will be different, but you'll do an inventory of these so you can pinpoint the ones that nag you the most. You'll cover everything from finances and chores to parenting, in-laws, friendships, and vacations.

You will be guided toward creative problem solving with your partner, so the two of you don't have to continuously reinvent the wheel or spend all of your energy on the same day-to-day problems. Through the Big Picture, you'll find that problem areas will instead become comfortable, agreed-upon routines. As a result, your creative energies will be freed up for your Big Picture dreams and visions, or for simply more fun and play.

Once you have your basics—the daily details—in order, the two of you will be ready to apply your mutual creativity to almost anything you can imagine:

- Planning new adventures and travels together
- Coordinating life change together such as a move or career change
- Starting and raising a family
- Offering your lifetime of skills to your community
- Living out your most delicious fantasy together

YOUR BIG PICTURE ADVENTURE

As you begin this adventure together, think about where you've been and where you might be headed. What has characterized your relationship up until this point in your lives, and how would you like your relationship to look a year from now?

The sixteen weeks to come could involve some of the deepest soul searching and some of the hardest work you may have done in your relationship. However, this hard work will make your lives easier, more intimate, and joyful for years to come.

EXERCISES

In the coming weeks as you do the exercises, each of you will reflect and write your own thoughts about each exercise in your journal, notebook, or Big Picture Partnering Workbook. Then you will come together to talk, create an activity, or dream together.

The Styles of Relating on Your Family Tree

In the following exercises you will have the opportunity to reflect on the relationship influences you experienced growing up, as well as those in your extended family history.

Each of you should individually make a sketch of your personal family tree. Begin with the branches closest to you, then your parents, grandparents, and great-grandparents. Don't forget to include members of blended families, especially stepparents.

Now look at your family tree. Identify which of the four styles of relating each of these couples models. (Some information might come from your direct experiences. Some may come from stories you've heard about these relatives.)

When you're finished, identify the style of relating you experience with your partner. This may be one clear style or a combination of two, three, or four styles.

Write about how satisfied you are with the current style(s) you experience in your relationship. Then explore the question: how would you like your relationship to be?

Bringing Your Relationship Experience Together

Reflect on how your relationship might be characterized according to the four styles presented during week 1.

Come together to share and compare your responses to this week's exercise.

First, place your family trees next to one another. Take turns describing the influences that come from your respective family histories.

Then, taking turns, tell one another what style or combination of styles you think typifies your relationship right now. Does your relationship most resemble the Traditional, Merged, Roommate, or Big Picture partnering style, or some combination of these four?

Talk about how your relationship has evolved over time. What were the various turning points when the underlying style of relating changed? Can you identify together what might have caused the change?

Talk together about whether or not you are satisfied with the style of relating that characterizes your relationship today.

Look at both your relationship as a whole, then various aspects of it (communication, conflict resolution, shared interests, sex life, household management, etc.).

Take turns talking about how you would like your relationship style to change.

In your journal, write down your responses and what you learned. Save what you've written to help you work toward becoming more loving and intimate partners in the coming weeks.

. . . .

Positively, Completely Yours

Maintaining positive feelings
between you

There are two Big Picture Essentials that continuously nourish your relationship. These two aspects of partnering are absolutely essential—like the air you breathe and the water that sustains the planet. During week 2, you will incorporate the first of these 10 Essentials: create and maintain positive feelings between you. In week 4 you will build its companion: talk together regularly, and take turns listening. If you implement these two Essentials whole-heartedly, your relationship will quickly and dramatically improve— no matter what your starting point.

Jaime and Jonathan are an example of a couple whose ups and downs were reflected in their inconsistent ability to nurture their relationship.

Jaime and Jonathan dated for two years before they married. Their first daughter was born within a year, and the second arrived within two years. Now, ten years later, Jaime runs her own research and consulting business from home. Jonathan is a middle manager at a local firm. They both agree that their relationship has been a committed one, but that it has run hot and cold ever since they were initially engaged. They talked about stretches of time when relating was smooth. Jaime volunteers,

> *During those times we get along, the house and schedules run well. We even have a lot of playfulness together, and with the kids. Of course, there's more sex!*

Jonathan adds:

> *And then we seem to hit a wall. I don't know why it keeps happening. One of us gets hurt or angry, or an old issue resurfaces. Then the cold war starts. Of course, I always think she starts it, but when it's over I know that isn't true. Sometimes it goes on for a few days, and sometimes it can stretch into two weeks. We each want the other person to apologize or warm up, but we are both pretty stubborn people. I don't even know what makes us get over it, but eventually we do. Maybe the problems go underground and we just go on. We really like each other, so eventually we give up the silent fight. I just wish we'd get over it sooner, and maybe get to the bottom of what is bugging us.*

Jaime says:

> *We'd both like to figure this out. It's tiring, and I get lonelier and lonelier every time it happens. I think this is because life is pretty demanding as the girls get older and our schedules include all of their*

activities as well as our own. The kids notice it too. I'd just like this to smooth out. Besides, he's my buddy—except when I'm upset and shut down or he's aloof and ignoring me.

HOW THE 5-TO-1 RATIO AFFECTS EVERY COUPLE

One of the ways couples have been studied over the last thirty years is in a laboratory setting, sometimes with observers taking notes behind a one-way mirror; at other times the couples are videotaped. In either approach, specific behaviors are then methodically counted and analyzed for their impact on the overall quality of the relationship. Ultimately, these studies search for ways to help couples maximize the positives that help relationships endure.

In the 1990s, such meticulous observation from a number of well-known research labs around the country yielded a harvest of data into the mainstream. At last there was a wealth of facts to back up the therapy and coaching methods many professionals were successfully, and sometimes not so successfully, using. We could finally say, "Here it is, folks! Here are twenty-some years of research data to back up our efforts to make relationships succeed. And, while relationships can be difficult or challenging, the tools to strengthen and make them better are not so difficult!"

One of the most consistently published and publicized professionals bringing forth this valuable data is John M. Gottman, Ph.D. Dr. Gottman is the cofounder and codirector of the Seattle Marital and Family Institute and professor of psychology at the University of Washington. He has studied thousands of couples and is able to predict, with 87 percent accuracy, which marriages are headed for divorce within three years. He is also 81 percent accurate in predicting which marriages will survive after seven to nine years. His research validates the need to create and maintain positive feelings between you.

As summarized in his book *Why Marriages Succeed or Fail,* one of the major factors in the endurance of relationships is the number of times certain behaviors are exhibited.

Gottman says:

> *The magic ratio is five-to-one. In other words, as long as there is five times as much positive feeling and interaction between husband and wife as there is negative, we found the marriage was likely to be stable. It was based on this ratio that we were able to predict whether couples were likely to divorce: in very unhappy couples, there tended to be more negative than positive interaction.*

He goes on to identify negative emotions as including anger, contempt, criticism, and defensiveness. The positive side of the equation is defined as showing interest, affection, appreciation, concern, and empathy; being accepting; joking around when it is fun for both; and sharing joy. In Gottman's research it doesn't matter how much negativity there is; what matters is that the positive far outshines it.

Such observation of couples finds that:

- Some couples fight like cats and dogs, and then kiss and make up—which can work.
- Some couples never fight. They only have discussions in a civilized and sedate manner. That also can work.
- When your styles of disagreement are different, both of you will need to learn a modified style.

Using the Big Picture approach, you will learn ways to present your disagreements and still be heard by your partner. You will also learn to listen to one another around difficult topics. Then, you will learn how to communicate creatively. But first, let's make your relationship rock-solid by reinforcing the positive feelings between you.

HOW THE 5-TO-1 RATIO MAKES YOUR BIG PICTURE PARTNERSHIP ROCK SOLID

Human beings are drawn to one another. When our antennae and honing mechanisms have not been damaged by early relationship experiences, we are naturally drawn to healthy relationships. We seek relationships for many reasons ranging from the intellectual to the spiritual, from the playful to the physical. If we pair this natural attraction to healthy relationships with self-awareness—we quickly know which people we want to pursue as friends, potential lovers, or even mates.

We all know that when we are in the honeymoon phase of a new relationship, we engage in our best behavior. We are "tuned in" and attentive to the other person as a new friendship or love relationship develops. During this honeymoon phase, positive interactions are typically very high. While we are not consciously aware of keeping the negatives low, we unconsciously try to show our best. This ratio of high positives in the beginning of any relationship is what keeps us coming back for more. When I asked Jaime and Jonathan to talk about what drew them together ten years ago, they took turns quickly coming up with substantial lists of things they liked about one another and enjoyed doing together. Jaime said:

> *He was always such a gentleman. Few other guys back then opened doors or brought flowers. It impressed me right off the bat! Then there*

was his sense of humor—gawd, could he make me laugh! He still does, when we are getting along.

Then Jonathan recalled:

She was always so upbeat and interested in knowing everything about me. She made me feel special. I loved the way she looked at me. She was good to my family, and they accepted her immediately.

"And what about intelligence, depth, and attraction?" I prompted, seeing that they were both good looking, fit, and smart. Jaime laughed:

Oh that! I take it for granted that he's smart. I couldn't be with a man unless he was a thinker. Jonathan is thoughtful, bright, and we share the same values. I've never stopped thinking he is a hunk!

Jonathan interjected:

I try to stay in shape. And, Jaime is downright beautiful, even in her jeans or sweats. I've always thought so. I guess I just don't tell her often enough anymore.

This statement became a segue in our conversation. Although a bit hesitant at first, Jaime and Jonathan began to link their earlier ability to show appreciation and to please one another with the drought in their current relationship. They realized how little they appreciated or tried to overtly please one another regularly anymore. Said Jaime,

I guess we just take one another for granted.

Jonathan joked, sounding somewhat melancholy:

I actually think I'm waiting for her to show me she's still interested in me—and still thinks I'm a hunk!—and smart, of course.

They were looking for new ideas to resolve their old "hot and cold" relating pattern. Big Picture partnering appealed to their desire to learn tools they could use together. While they both referred to a need to resolve some old issues, the first essential lesson was to bring back a continuous positive feeling between them. They not only needed to create, but also to maintain positive feelings. There had been many positive interactions during the early years. They knew how to do this; they just needed to put into practice what they already knew. This was their first assignment.

Just like we know that during the honeymoon couples put their best foot forward, we also know that the longer we interact with another person, the closer we become, and the more we reveal aspects of our personality, attitudes, and behavior. As the honeymoon wanes, we gradually feel more comfortable revealing our warts. We let down our hair; we let down our guard. And, sadly, the longer we know someone—especially the one we are closest to—the more often we take one another for granted. It is not unusual for people to treat colleagues and acquaintances with more kindness and respect than those they live with and love the most. It is not uncommon to see friends or workmates receiving the best time, the most high quality interactions, while mate and family members receive the leftovers.

You may see yourself in some of the following examples of couples who take one another for granted or put other things before their relationship:

> *Will frequently comes home late from work, and I'm disappointed when he misses a great dinner I've prepared. Sometimes he even forgets the kids' baseball games. They are always so proud when he shows up, but I can tell they try not to get their hopes up, because we just can't count on him these days. He puts work first.*
>
> Sarah, married nine years to Will

Carl was such a gentleman when we first knew one another. He'd not only open doors and spend time with me, but he actually talked to me every day—like he really wanted to and enjoyed it. Now all he does is joke about my weight or talk sarcastically about my work. He gets lost in the television or some household chore when I want more time for talk and affection.

Ramona, married eleven years to Carl

Lynette cleans house every night, long after I've gone to bed. I feel like she puts the chores before me—and I feel ignored. She always says she'll come to bed early, and I know she feels guilty. But she doesn't change her behavior.

Paul, married thirteen years to Lynette

At work, Mike is a playful, funny, flamboyant, intelligent conversationalist. He keeps his coworkers laughing and his customers love him. But at home he's grumpy and tired. He doesn't interact with me or the kids except to complain or scold.

Marilyn, married sixteen years to Mike

Marilyn is kind and talkative to her friends on the phone every night, but when I approach her—with a hug or pat—she shrugs her shoulders and acts disinterested in me. It hurts.

Mike, married sixteen years to Marilyn

My flamboyance is what attracted Josh to me and drew him out initially. But now it embarrasses him when I'm outgoing in public. He gets angry about it when we get home and teases me about how I act and talk around his friends. Sometimes to cover up his embarrassment, he mimics me in public or puts me down. When we get home, he'll ignore my affectionate advances by shutting down and claiming he's tired.

Barbara, married eight years to Josh

When we take one another for granted, common negative interactions that develop are shaming, blaming, judging, anger, and criticism. Other forms of common negative interactions include teasing, sarcasm, ignoring, not listening, trying to "get a rise" out of your partner, not following through on an agreement, avoiding interactions—such as lovemaking or important discussions—through excessive alcohol use, excessive time spent on hobbies or sports, or excessive work. The most obvious forms of negative interactions include any form of blatant abuse, be it verbal, emotional, physical, or sexual.

When we take our loved ones for granted—when we put our love relationship last on the list of priorities—love, and the ultimate success of our most important relationship, is at stake. All of the above are examples of how negative interactions can erode any love relationship if positive interactions and feelings do not outweigh them.

In Big Picture partnering, couples create and maintain a positive feeling toward one another at all times. They do this by actively upholding a positive, nurturing, and loving relationship environment through their daily actions toward their partner, no matter what their partner is doing. In keeping with the research on successful relationships, Big Picture partners maintain a 5-to-1 Ratio or better of positive to negative interactions. This is their insurance policy, the emotional savings account that sustains them during times of stress. It is their consistent investment that reflects the high priority they give their partnership.

In Big Picture partnering, if you have one argument, or one tense or stressful interaction within a day or a week, you need at least five positive interactions within that same period of time; if you have four difficult, heated, or argumentative interactions, you need twenty positive interactions.

A positive interaction may be a hug, a pat on the back, bringing home flowers, making a nice dinner, doing a favor, making love, saying something nice about that person, being willing to resolve a difficult situation through staying "present" in a conversation, and so on. Positive interactions that outweigh negative ones are defined as those considered positive in the eyes of you and your partner.

Big Picture partners know that problems will be addressed so they don't have to focus all their attention on resolving difficulties all of the time. Big Picture partners know they can schedule time to attend to any difficulty. They also know that if they are feeling good about their partnership, difficulties and disagreements seem smaller—so they keep positive interactions flowing all of the time.

PLEASE YOUR PARTNER AND INCREASE YOUR PLEASURE TOGETHER

Sometimes couples are in great upheaval or pain. They may have significant issues that they are attempting to resolve. They may mistakenly imagine that if they discuss these repeatedly and constantly this will help. They sometimes come in to my office having argued and knitted a topic over and over so much they no longer do anything pleasant together. In this situation, a couple's positive-to-negative ratio is totally unbalanced, and their relationship nourishment is at the famine level. These factors inhibit resolution.

Under such circumstances it is sometimes difficult to refocus your-selves as a couple, to reverse the positive-to-negative ratio. Be reas-sured that the issues will be attended to in time—using the communication tools we will discuss later in future chapters. But first you must nourish the relationship through expanding the positive interactions between you. When couples are willing to lay down their arms, put fights on hold, and increase the positive interactions, they usually feel more connected again. They make the first step, together, toward reconnection.

Your relationship may be stronger and less stressed than the couples I have just described. Even if that's the case, make sure the nurturance level in your relationship is high. Without positive feelings, we may not see the good, we have less desire to give or work on problematic areas, we succumb to waiting for the other person to change first. A nourishing environment of positive feelings gives us the energy to deal with situations that arise. What appeared to be a big issue or problem suddenly seems doable, smaller, less threatening. We feel more sponta-neous and playful. Our relationship feels sweeter, juicier.

All people know what to do to please their partner. Each of us has a wealth of experience. Once the honeymoon is over, however, some people act as if they forgot, don't know, or don't remember what makes their partner happy, even though they have observed happy, excited, or pleased responses at other times during their relationship. When I challenge couples on this point, asking them to make lists or say out loud the things that please their partner, they come up with at least four or five things they are sure of. This is a start. And, if they have forgotten what pleases their partner, I encourage them to ask.

When you go out of your way to do something that pleases your partner, both can reap the benefits.

In Big Picture partnering, partners are encouraged to have a healthy repertoire of "positives" they can do and interchange regularly, so that positive interactions become like breathing air —natural, regular, and easy, always nourishing the two people involved.

THE DO NOT FIGHT RULE

In the next few weeks, I am going to ask those of you who fight about issues that remain unresolved to stop. For now. If your fights are unresolved, it means you do not yet have the tools to be successful together. Big Picture partners work toward mutual success. I want you to be successful. During the next fourteen weeks, you will learn the tools to tackle your unresolved problems and issues while you also learn to be more creative together. Built into the coming weeks of Big Picture partnering are safe ways to talk about difficult topics in new ways. For the time being, bite your tongues, write in your journal, go for a walk, and, most importantly, make a pact together to learn how to communicate better—to communicate for resolution and creativity in the coming weeks.

E X E R C I S E S

Awareness of Positives and Feeling Loved

At the beginning of this week, write in your journals or workbooks. As you write, ask yourselves: What is the positive-to-negative ratio in my partnership now? How do I contribute to its being high or low? If I notice I am withholding something—affection, time, attention, sex, talk, play, or anything else I know would please my partner—why is that? What are my concerns or motivations for not keeping the good feelings flowing? Am I waiting for my partner to go first? What attitudes and behaviors do I need to change to see or do this differently? What could I do (no matter what my partner is doing) to enhance this base of good feeling within my partnership?

Refine your awareness of what pleases you and your partner as you continue to individually write in your journals. Write about those actions that make you feel cared about or loved.

Then contemplate what you think satisfies your partner. What makes each of us feel loved is unique. Often, we assume that what makes us feel loved also makes our partner feel loved. Ask yourself, am I willing to learn from my partner how to express my love in a way that they can appreciate most?

Thank your partner for the specific things they do to make you feel loved. For example, you might say, "These past few weeks I've really appreciated you taking charge of the kids when I first come home from the office. That down time really helps me to regroup and be more present for the rest of the evening. Thanks. I love you and look forward to having more relaxing evenings together."

Throughout this week and the next fourteen weeks, pay attention to how your partner pleases you. Make a note in your journal or workbook at the end of each day; call it your "Everything you did that I appreciated today" list. (Share your list with your partner from time to time.)

Then, come together as partners and share your reflections. Make a pact to increase the degree of good feelings between you by each contributing generously.

Expanding Your Loving

Another day this week, take turns sharing what makes each of you feel loved by the other. Then, create and give each other a list of three or four additional things that you would like your partner to do for you. Make things concrete. For example, you might say, "I really enjoy when you arrange the babysitter and pick the movie on our night out." Or, "When you call me during the day just to say hello, I feel very cared for." Or, "I love it when you tease me with your toes under the tablecloth when we're eating in a nice restaurant."

This week, work on expanding the positive—your love repertoire—together.

. . . .

Our Do Not Fight Pact

We, _____ *and* _____
agree to discontinue fighting about hot topics, big problems, and unresolved issues during the coming weeks while we practice becoming more intimate partners. We do this knowing we will have ample opportunity to discuss these issues—with improved communication ability—in weeks nine through sixteen.

_____   _____
Signed   Signed

_____   _____
Date   Date

· ·

Nurturing Yourselves

Deepening your individuality
deepens your relationship

Learning how to "build the muscles" of a strong, mature adult self is crucial for Big Picture partners. It is only when you can relate to each other from a mature place that you can create a mutually fulfilling life.

In week 3 we're going to explore the importance of establishing a solid foundation of individuality, of developing a solid, whole adult self, so that you can become more intimate, creative, and connected. We'll also talk about how you can achieve and exercise the muscles of this adult self, and improve your relationship dramatically by doing so.

OUR HUMAN ABILITY TO EVOLVE

Human beings are remarkably diverse creatures. We are imperfect, yet extraordinary in many ways. Our diversity, idiosyncrasies, and uniqueness are hallmarks of individual development. The development of our unique self is impacted by genetics, culture, upbringing, and life experience. In the early phases of our life, these coalesce into what becomes the core of our individual identity. That identity then continues to blossom over many decades. Such personal growth happens when we are curious and flexible, and when we accept challenges and engage in new experiences. On the other hand, identity becomes static or rigid when we are inflexible, isolated, or fearful of change.

Scientists and psychologists used to believe that development occurred only in childhood—that by the time we arrived at early adulthood our personalities and patterns were pretty much set in stone. They thought that if a person had a certain type of early experience, it foretold the positive or negative outcomes of their adulthood. Sometimes we find that this does appear to be true; however, current science and recent longitudinal studies of human development paint a very different picture of our capacity for growth and change. We now know that we can change and evolve throughout our lives. As medical science keeps our bodies in better shape, people well into their nineties and beyond continue to have the capacity to evolve as individuals—psychologically, mentally, interpersonally. While we never reach a state of perfection, we do continue to evolve. So we can think of ourselves, at every stage of our lives, as works in progress.

This ability to continuously evolve is a wonderful aspect of our human nature. It means it is never too late—you are never too old or too stuck—to change, for yourself and for your relationship. It means that old habits may die hard, but they can be replaced with new thoughts, perceptions, and even behaviors. It may take hard work—or not. You may have already made many changes. It may take some education or new resources. It may take a great desire to learn something new or do something in a new way. But any of this is possible for you, just because you are one of the remarkable species called human.

DISCOVERING AND DEVELOPING YOUR UNIQUE ADULT SELF

Exploring and developing our uniqueness—the characteristics, talents, and values that define who we are as individuals—is the essential task of growing up. What we develop in this process is our Adult self. This is the self that defines who we are, what we share with others, and what we bring to our partnering and family life. It is our responsibility to continuously nurture and develop this self over the course of our lifetime.

Your unique creativity allows you to express yourself in the world. This self-expression may be manifest in how you parent, teach, write, or paint. It may be in the making of wonderful food or in the garden you grow. Your self-expression may come out in how you dress, talk, dance, walk, sing, or play. Think about it. You have the opportunity, and the choice, to express yourself every moment of every day. It is just like the choice to love. You can hide yourself under a bushel basket, or you can take risks to become just a little more wildly, joyously, fully creative—and thus, more fully you. As you both do so, your relationship will reap the benefits.

CHARACTERISTICS OF HAPPY, HEALTHY ADULTS

Within our Western culture, we are among the first generations to have many opportunities so we are the first to consciously seek happiness. What encompasses or promotes happiness or contentment in life is a relatively simple list of characteristics. Sometimes life circumstances, our personal struggles with desire, or the flashiness of advertising and media confuse us. Yet, strip these away and the building blocks of contentment are relatively accessible. Throughout childhood, adolescence, and early adulthood, we develop the knowledge, capabilities, and values that become the template upon which we build our characters. The following characteristics contribute to ongoing personal growth, contentment, and happiness in one's adult life.

Develop self-awareness and take time for self-reflection

Develop vigorous curiosity about life

Develop, balance, and strengthen masculine and feminine characteristics

Develop the ability to empathize and express compassion

Develop and enjoy close and satisfying relationships

Develop deeper meaning in your life

Happy, healthy adults have a balance
of these aspects in their lives.

DEVELOPING YOUR SELF-AWARENESS AND SPENDING TIME IN SELF-REFLECTION

Self-awareness is the ability to observe our own actions and reactions; self-reflection taps memory and hones an ability to evaluate our behaviors and responses. Such inner observation helps you to make choices about the effectiveness or your pursuits and the success of your actions, your emotional responses, and communications—especially with those you love.

Awareness and self-reflection are also connected to deeper levels of knowing oneself, sometimes known as the intuition, inner voice, or subconscious mind. In everyday life, sometimes we have little time to tap into this powerful asset.

It takes a little time to become self-aware. Contemplating quietly, meditating, listening to wise counsel, reading self-help or philosophical books, writing in a journal, and focusing your thoughts while you run or swim or bike are some ways to hone this necessary skill. I recommend that you give yourself thirty to sixty minutes each day to become quiet and reflect, to tap into your center of calm, deeper wisdom, and greatest dreams.

DEVELOPING A VIGOROUS CURIOSITY ABOUT LIFE

Having the ability to be adaptable goes a long way in life, especially with current longevity. Developing a curiosity about all that life has to offer keeps us flexible, and feeds our creative juices. A perspective of curiosity helps us accept the many changes that our fast-paced world demands.

Studies show that when we are deeply curious about something, we get lost in the moment. That lost-in-the-moment feeling is akin to contentment or happiness. In addition, the flexibility that comes with an open-minded, open-hearted, flexible approach to life helps us to become like trees with deep roots—the winds may buffet us about a bit, but we do not topple.

DEVELOPING, BALANCING, AND STRENGTHENING YOUR MASCULINE AND FEMININE ASPECTS

We struggle to achieve a comfortable balance in many aspects of our internal and external lives: between our social and contemplative sides, our work and personal life, earning a living and giving back to the community. Attaining such balance strengthens us. Balancing the masculine and feminine characteristics within our personality is also strengthening. Studies show that individuals who have integrated high masculine and high feminine aspects in their personalities do better in life. Specifically, they have higher self-esteem and function better in society than individuals who have very low masculine-feminine aspects.

Developing strong masculine and feminine aspects does not mean becoming overly macho or overly sweet and sensitive. Instead, it is allowing yourself to explore the breadth of emotions and behaviors commonly known to both men and women. It means exploring this continuum to find how you best express yourself in the world on all levels—physically, mentally, emotionally, and socially—without down-playing or taming any of your talents or urges. When two people bring this strength to partnering, you get a blend of qualities that enrich a relationship, shake you out of rigid role models, and make for lively interchange of ideas and creativity.

DEVELOPING YOUR ABILITY TO EMPATHIZE WITH AND EXPRESS COMPASSION FOR OTHERS

This characteristic refers to what is commonly called emotional intelligence. It enables you to move out of your personal realm and into the realm of the interpersonal. Empathy is the ability to know or imagine what another person is feeling or experiencing, to step outside your personal experience and see or hear or imagine how another must feel.

Compassion takes empathy one step further. It is the ability to respond to another person's feelings or experience appropriately. This means sharing their joy, success, laughter, and glee. Compassion means caring for others when they are down, hurting, or in pain. It means sharing with another the struggle of change or growth when life circumstances are challenging.

It may seem obvious that empathy and compassion benefit not only you but everyone around you, especially in your partnering and family life. Empathy and compassion are not about what you imagine, need, or want. They are about what the other person feels, needs, and wants. Empathy is knowing that another person has a birthday and loves to celebrate. Compassion is choosing and offering just the right gift—one that you know the other person would love or cherish.

Although some people are innately better at empathizing and being compassionate, these are worthwhile attributes to develop for you and everyone around you, both at home and at work. You might practice putting yourself in another person's shoes a few minutes each day. Practice listening to what they say they are feeling. If they don't say feeling words, observe their body language and tone of voice, and listen to what they need.

ENJOYING CLOSE AND SATISFYING RELATIONSHIPS

One of the most important requirements for life satisfaction is the development of your capacity to have close, intimate relationships. Women tend to develop strong, interconnected webs of friendship and support, while men tend to create networks of collaborators through work and activities. In our country, 86 percent of all people are married at least once in their lifetime. Of those who divorce or break up, a great number go on to either live together or marry again. Since most of us have an inner drive to seek a partner, learning to stay connected and to develop intimacy with another person is nearly a guarantee of contentment, satisfaction, and happiness in one's life.

It makes sense that developing our capacity for human connection sustains our life and makes us happier. Since our culture teaches us to seek happiness, doing our part to learn how to be close and stay joyfully connected is crucial.

DEVELOPING A DEEPER MEANING IN YOUR LIFE

Finally, people who do best in life, who report the greatest involvement, who are the most engaged and engaging, have some way of expressing their life's purpose or meaning. Their values and beliefs are aligned with their life choices, and thus their activities and interactions are infused with meaning. For many, this higher purpose or deeper meaning is grounded in a spiritual or religious practice. Each of us discovers our own sense of purpose and meaning in life. What seems universally apparent, however, is the need to explore this part of our life. There are numerous religious, spiritual, and philosophical traditions that can offer guidance. Personal contemplation, introspection, and journal writing; music, literature, dance, or creative pursuits; and the study of the natural world can also inspire you to find the connections that give a higher purpose and a deeper meaning to your everyday life.

HOW DO YOU STRENGTHEN THE HEALTHY ASPECTS OF YOUR ADULT SELF?

In the previous section I highlighted those characteristics and pursuits that define a healthy, mature adult self. Let's look at how we go about strengthening the muscles of this self.

A helpful way of teaching couples to distinguish their healthy adult behaviors from unhealthy interactions comes out of Transactional Analysis. TA is a school of psychological thinking, out of which comes the concept of the Parent/Adult/Child selves within each of us. This simple approach to the human personality will:

- Provide you with an understanding of the responses and reactions that help or hinder your relationships
- Empower you with options to change negative responses to your partner and respond in ways that are appropriate to the situation

Once you can distinguish your healthy adult behaviors from unhealthy interactions, your skills in communicating and interacting will quickly expand. What made you feel stuck before will change when you have a repertoire of healthy behavioral choices. I think of expanding this repertoire of adult behaviors as muscle building; sometimes we all need a personal trainer to teach us new strategies and keep us on track. Big Picture partnering, with its 10 Essentials, is part of your personal training to help you become a rock-solid couple. The parent/adult/child model that comes out of Transactional Analysis is an integral part of your training.

In Big Picture partnering, your ability to recognize and quickly change or rectify your verbal and behavioral responses to one another enhances the solidity and longevity of your relationship. Understanding the parent/adult/child states will help you in this regard.

THE PARENT/ADULT/CHILD MODEL

Take a look at the diagram on the next page. This view of the human personality shows that at any one time, we experience one of three basic selves: the parent, the adult, and the child. In addition, the parent and child selves each have a positive and an unhealthy or wounded aspect that will be further described. Remember, becoming aware of these selves that reside within you, and developing a strong adult self, are the ultimate goals. When you achieve them, you develop emotional flexibility. The more resilient your personality becomes:

- The more flexible you will be in navigating between these selves
- The more options you will have in your communications
- The more you will be able to partner in a healthy way

Let me describe the parent, adult, and child selves to you in greater detail.

THE PARENT SELF

Carole and Bob, married eleven years, have a natural ability to spread good will and warmth to everyone in their lives. Their affection for their rambunctious two-year-old twins, Alec and Tim, is obvious. Everyone would say they are fantastic parents. One parent is always watching over their active boys, gently wiping a runny nose, soothing tears, distracting them when they take one another's toys, rocking

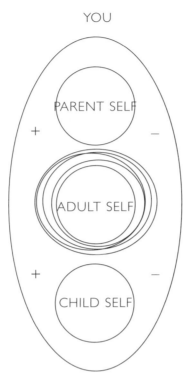

YOU

PARENT SELF

$+$ $-$

ADULT SELF

$+$ $-$

CHILD SELF

Your Parent/Adult/Child selves

them when they get sleepy, singing and telling them bedtime stories. Observing Carole and Bob, you'd note they are just as kind to the family pet—a big, yellow Lab named Max, who guards over the boys patiently as they crawl all over his body.

Bob and Carole started their family in their late thirties, so both sets of parents are older, and Carole's are in need of much attention and physical care. Carole and Bob share these responsibilities with her three siblings, who comment on how loving they both are to mom and dad. In fact, Bob and Carole are as caring and nurturing toward Carole's parents as they are with Alec and Tim.

The parent self has two aspects—one has positive responses and the other has negative or unhealthy responses. You developed these positive and unhealthy behaviors and attitudes through observation of parent role models when you were a child. For all of us, this is learned through interaction with parents, grandparents, aunts, uncles, teachers, and other adults in our childhood. As we grow older, the behaviors and attitudes of the parent figures around us are unconsciously internalized, until they seem like "a part of us."

If you look at the diagram of the parent self, the positive aspects of this state are nurturing and caring. These are the way we care for a child, a pet, the very sick, or the very old.

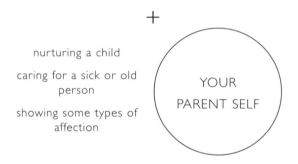

+

nurturing a child

caring for a sick or old person

showing some types of affection

YOUR PARENT SELF

Some positive parent aspects

In partnering relationships, problems arise when we try to parent our partner. When we do nurture another adult out of the parental state, it typically feels condescending or like being treated like a child. This is different than healthy nurturing or caring for a partner from our adult self, which I will describe later in this chapter.

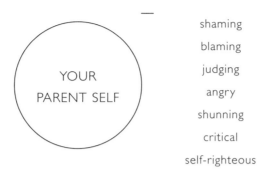

YOUR
PARENT SELF

shaming

blaming

judging

angry

shunning

critical

self-righteous

Some negative or critical parent aspects

The negative or unhealthy aspect of the parent self is called the Critical Parent. The critical parent embodies the characteristics you have internalized that are not only critical, but also shaming, blaming, judging, self-righteous, or angry. It may be spoken criticism or a silent judgmental vibe. Sometimes this is demonstrated by giving someone the cold shoulder, showing a look of disgust, rolling the eyes in utter dismay, or even shunning a person for a time. You may recognize this as pointing an angry finger at others, or even pointing it at yourself. Carole and Bob's experiences provide an example. In talking about her husband, Carole said:

> *Bob is sometimes his own worst enemy. He's a wonderful man, and—he's a perfectionist. I can tell when he's let himself down. He'll become quiet and sullen. Once in awhile he'll pick on me, or become critical of the twins. It's not usually like him. But it does remind me of how his dad always snaps at his wife—Bob's mom—and talks down about anyone who doesn't follow the old man's rules for how to live life. Once you've crossed Grandpa, it takes a long time to get back in his good graces. He sure knows how to make a person feel worthless! I*

think that's why Bob has become so loving in his own life—not wanting to be like his father in that way. Yet, it comes out when he doesn't live up to his own expectations. I'll find out later that he overlooked someone at the office, or someone he supervises made a mistake and Bob feels he handled it poorly. He can get himself coming and going.

Just like Bob, many people are their own worst critical parent—they need no one else to blame them or point a shaming finger at them. They do it to themselves, silently and internally. It is best to spend no time in the critical parent state, because it is demeaning, detrimental to self-esteem, and harmful to any relationship. Instead, I will show you the benefits and behaviors of developing a strong adult self.

> As you reflect on the parent self and complete the exercises at the end of this chapter, consider: What behaviors and attitudes did I learn from adults around me as a child, and how do I use them in negative ways with my partner (and other people around me) now?

THE CHILD SELF

When Bob comes home from work, many evenings he and Carole get down on the living room floor to wrestle and play with their two-year-old twin boys, who squeal with delight at this physical contact. Carole and Bob delight in the affectionate tussle, laughing and making silly noises right along with their boys. Then they end this little pre-dinner ritual by sprawling out in a circle end to end with each one's head on another one's belly—for belly laughing and giggling until they wind down. Bob says:

It is such a great way to reconnect and switch gears at the end of a long work day. The boys calm down. My head is no longer at work. Carole and I have touched and hugged, and we've all connected once again. No matter what our days have been like, we are all there together, and it feels great.

The child self is frequently referred to as the Inner Child. The positive characteristics of an adult's inner child are the playful, joyful, generously loving, sometimes mischievous ways we can be when we feel safe and secure with another person or group of people. Maybe we enter this childlike, innocent, playful state with our children. Sometimes we may get silly or mischievous with our mate, or with our friends when we are goofing around. It is wonderful to be playfully childlike when we feel safe and secure with those around us.

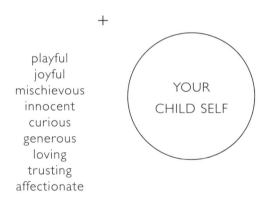

+

playful
joyful
mischievous
innocent
curious
generous
loving
trusting
affectionate

YOUR
CHILD SELF

Some positive child aspects

The negative experience of the child self that we carry inside, even in adulthood—is sometimes called the Wounded Child. It is not really bad; rather, it is the part of yourself that got hurt as a child. It reflects how you responded to being hurt by those you loved. If we investigate the feelings and behaviors of our wounded child, we find a direct reproduction of what we felt, what we thought, and how we behaved when we were hurt in our childhood.

Bob talks about how his father's behavior influenced him as a child.

> *My dad was a heavy drinker when we were growing up. He was a loving man, but then he could turn on you when he had too much to drink. Because we boys were supposed to be little men, when he yelled at me, I'd try not to show it, but I'd feel like dying on the inside! I never was sure I pleased him, and I always wanted him to be proud of me.*
>
> *Now, I know I'm hard on myself, and others, sometimes. And when my boss is upset with me or Carole hurts my feelings or doesn't give me enough attention—especially since we've had the twins—once in awhile I have to work hard not to shut down and withdraw inside. It's a challenge because neither of them are really like my dad, but I find myself doing the same old behaviors once in awhile. I'm working on it.*

Carole pipes up:

> *I, on the other hand, if my parents, sisters, or school friends hurt me, the tears just flowed. Inside, I was always trying to figure out what happened; it always seemed so unfair, and I wanted to make it right— to make sense out of it. Then I'd have to talk it over with the person who had hurt me until we got reconnected. I still have to do that now! When Bob or someone hurts me, I still feel badly. But then I try to figure it out and always want to talk it over and reconcile with the other person as soon as possible.*

Bob added:

Boy does she ever! In our relationship it's a good thing though, because my instinct is to withdraw, and Carole won't let me—she's got to talk it out. She never let's us go to bed angry or disconnected. I have an older brother who is just the opposite. Dad would criticize Mom or one of us, and Arnold would be ready for a fight—always ready to take Dad on to defend himself or any one of us. They could really get into it. Arnold still is known for his temper whenever he thinks something is an injustice or he sees an underdog.

When we think of the possible responses to being hurt as a child, there is a whole continuum of options. If you have children, observe their behaviors when they are hurt by playmates, siblings, teachers, or even by you as a parent.

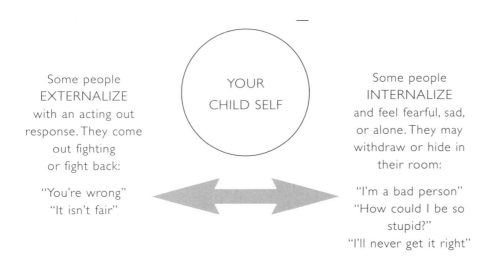

Some people
EXTERNALIZE
with an acting out
response. They come
out fighting
or fight back:

YOUR
CHILD SELF

Some people
INTERNALIZE
and feel fearful, sad,
or alone. They may
withdraw or hide in
their room:

"You're wrong"
"It isn't fair"

"I'm a bad person"
"How could I be so
stupid?"
"I'll never get it right"

A continuum of some wounded child responses you may experience.

Some children feel very sad or defeated when their feelings get hurt by their parents. They shut down and run to their rooms and hide in the closet, or may pull the covers over their heads. They may cry. They may have thoughts about how bad they are, how alone they feel. Often children whose feelings are hurt may come out kicking, screaming, and hollering. To be hurt makes them mad, and they want to lash out. These children don't feel sad—they feel angry! They may think the other person is "unfair" or wrong or bad. Still other children simply don't move when their feelings are hurt. They shut down and "go away" inside while their body stays "present." They may be feeling sadness or defeat—or they may think how wrong or stupid the other person is and how unfairly life is treating them at the moment.

Sometimes people will describe the one way they responded to being hurt in childhood. Other people describe two major ways they responded. One way of responding may have occurred frequently with a particular parent or sibling; the other may have happened with schoolmates or other people outside the home. Sometimes people describe responding with sadness as a young child, and then lashing out angrily as they entered adolescence.

> As you reflect on the child self in the exercises at the end of this chapter answer the question: "How did I respond—in my behaviors—when I was hurt as a young child—and how do I react similarly in my thoughts, feelings, and behaviors when I am hurt by my partner (or anyone else) now?"

THE ADULT SELF

Imagine the diagram below as a large sphere called Your Adult Self—the healthy space or state that you, as an adult, get to interact from. When describing the adult self, I often hold my arms in the air as though I were gently embracing a large, three-dimensional orb. The diameter and inner space connote the spaciousness of the adult self; the circumference suggests limits beyond which thoughts, actions, words, and experiences become too extreme or are too out-of-the-adult bounds.

The muscles of your adult self evolve and strengthen over time. These "muscles" make you feel resilient and ready to handle life's joys and challenges.

Some people react negatively when they think of becoming "adult" or "mature." They want to cling to the vestiges of childhood and maybe even childish behaviors. They misunderstand true adult-hood, which is not limiting or stifling. In fact, it is freeing because it encompasses so much of one's life experience and learning. Most mature adults are far less self-conscious, self-doubting, or concerned with petty things than they were while growing up or in their early adult years. Maturity can bring a lightness of heart and the beginnings of wisdom, so imagine that the adult self is spacious! There is room for a great breadth of feelings and behaviors.

The edges of your adult self help you determine what is healthy or unhealthy. Going beyond these edges lets you know you are too manic or too "in the pits" with depression. As a healthy adult, you know when you are too full of rage or too silent and withdrawn. Within the spaciousness of adulthood, you know and accept your strengths and weaknesses, you discriminate what you like and don't like. As a healthy adult, you know what you know, you know what you don't know, and you know where and when to look outside for information, help, or advice. As a healthy adult, you are not too humble, and you are not too arrogant. You are willing to learn, to grow, and to accept this process as a part of being human. You want to succeed; you know that perfection does not exist. It is that feeling you have when you walk down the street and you feel all right with the world.

The diagram on the next page puts all these selves together.

As we mature, the healthy adult self is the state we should strive to be in most of the time when we interact with other adults—especially with our partner. The only exceptions are when both adults are feeling playful, young, and safe with one another, or when one is in a nurturing parent self and interacting with a child, the elderly, someone who is ill, or an animal.

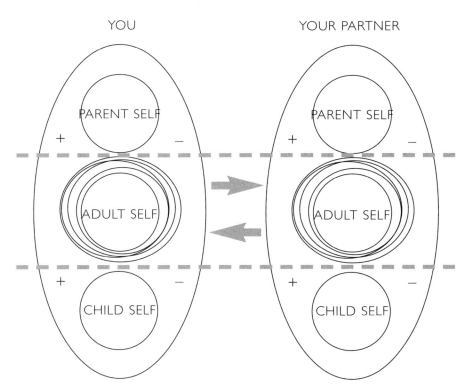

Your Parent/Adult/Child selves
As two strong, resilient adult selves connect and communicate,
their creativity, intimacy, and satisfaction are enhanced.

In learning to think, feel, and behave as your adult self, there are two strategies to become aware of:

- Avoid bouncing back and forth between your child self and parent self, so you don't bypass your adult self.

- Allow your adult self to care for your child self, so that you don't look to your partner (and others) to do so.

How to Avoid Bypassing Your Adult Self

Once we become aware of the three selves within us, we feel best when we're being our adult self. We realize that we've been there, done that with regard to the hurtful parts of childhood, so why continue to revisit them by choice? And the critical parent self just isn't very nice to be around.

As you do the exercises at the end of this chapter and become more aware of your internal selves, you may notice just how much time you actually spend being the critical parent or the wounded child. When I ask couples to nonjudgmentally observe their parent/adult/child selves for a week or two, many of them are astounded to discover how much time they spend as the wounded child and how often they bounce back and forth between the wounded child and the critical parent, feeling hurt and sad, then beating themselves up, then feeling bad once again! Bob talks about his experience with this pattern—and how Carole and his friends help him overcome it.

> *Sometimes I'll do something I'm ashamed of, then withdraw like I did when I was little and Dad yelled at me. Right there will be that critical Dad voice rubbing it in, telling me how stupid I am. I've learned to get back to my more reasonable adult self as I've worked on changing this pattern. It sure feels better. I spent eighteen years listening to Dad berate*

us all from time to time—I don't want to do that to myself for the rest of my life!

Now I try to forgive myself for screwing up and talk myself through what I know is the truth—that everyone makes mistakes. I have a couple of guy friends I can talk things over with, especially when it's work related. We are serious for a bit and then we joke around and kid each other. Of course they'll kid me about it later, but I feel very accepted by them. It's a guy thing.

Carole's good at helping me put things in perspective, too. We stay on track together. We're good for one another in that way. I know I help her when she does things she's not proud of as well.

Like Bob, you may also have a pattern of bypassing your adult self at times and reverting to your critical parent—or your wounded child. Or you may find that when you do become your adult self, your repertoire of behaviors and verbal responses is small and unused—like muscles that are unused. If this is the case, Big Picture partnering and conversations with your partner will enable you to exercise your "muscles" as you develop your adult self. Practicing the 10 Essentials of Big Picture partnering will give you a larger, more flexible set of tools, skills, behaviors, and responses.

Every adult I have worked with has at least a small adult-self repertoire. You may easily slip into your repertoire around colleagues, coworkers, friends, or new acquaintances. We all use our best adult behavior in public; it is in our private, most personal relationships—with romantic partners and family—that all of our childhood and critical parent buttons get pushed and we forget to stay adult.

It is the task of maturing to grow your adult self and to spend almost all of your time interacting from within it. If you discover you have weak adult "muscles," start by identifying the muscles that you have. Then look around for positive adult role modeling. How do other adults behave, interact, and communicate when they are at their best? A key phrase I like to offer people is to always behave with "grace and dignity." Everyone immediately understands grace, dignity, and respect. These concepts summarize and encompass the essence of the adult self.

In addition, I recommend rereading the basic requirements for developing a healthy adult self at the beginning of this chapter. Talk to friends. Find a mentor or coach. Observe and interact with other people you admire. Read biographies and autobiographies about people you admire for their grace, their dignity, and the respect they inspire. Participate in your church or community. Give to others who are less fortunate. Gravitate to people and activities that challenge your thinking and your emotional and spiritual growth. All of these exercise the muscles of healthy adulthood.

If you have not yet learned enough adult behaviors and responses, it is not too late, regardless of your age. If both you and your partner work to strengthen your adult selves, you will have the inner strength —the adult "muscles"—to tackle the Big Picture adventure as you continue to build your rock-solid partnering in the coming weeks.

Sometimes It's Hard to Be an Adult

Sometimes our adult self may need something as silly as a refresher in table manners or social graces to feel competent in the larger world, or new ways to talk to the boss or a coworker. Sometimes we need to know the boundaries of sexuality, or how to stay adult in heated discussions or arguments. Trying to resolve stressful grown-up matters— your partner's insensitive behavior or your hurt feelings when your partner seems unaware of your needs—is futile when one or both of you become childish or critical.

Let's look at how to handle emotions from within the adult self.

Handling Emotions as an Adult

According to TA, our parent, adult, and child selves always exist. We carry each within us forever. They do not grow up or go away. Even if you successfully strengthen your adult muscles, in stressful or trigger situations you may still revert to the behaviors of a wounded child or the critical parent. The adult emotions are appropriate and effective. The wounded child emotions are valid as well; they are just not very effective in getting you what you want and need in your adult life. The critical parent should be avoided altogether.

In couple relationships, if one or both individuals try to get their needs met when in a wounded child state, this can be damaging and frustrating. First, both people run the risk of being hurt and wounded by their mate. Second, if one person flips into the critical parent role, there will be a power imbalance and more hurt will ensue from being criticized, shamed, blamed, or judged. If both people are feeling little, then neither one gets comforted or has their needs met.

Ivan, married four years to Marlene, talks about how the child and parent selves play out in their relationship at times.

> When I'm feeling vulnerable, I sure can't show it around Marlene. She expects me always to be strong and comes on with a lecture in a very stern voice about all the ways I could improve my lot. I end up feeling like she's trying to be my mother. I know she doesn't want this either, but it leaves me feeling unmanly, and extremely angry with her in the long run. She says she feels trapped by my behavior when I'm needy like that and doesn't know how to respond in a positive way. She tries, but we both lose out.

Penny, who has been living with Mike for nine months, says the two of them are also grappling with the parent/child predicament:

I feel so out of sorts these days and I don't think Mike knows what to do, so he just goes silent on me. I cry and make a scene when he's not home on time, and I miss him or am worried about him. I feel so immature, yet I can't keep myself from acting this way. I know everything is okay between us, but moving in together is more stressful than I could have imagined.

When George and Les, who have been committed partners for six years, have more than the usual stress at work, they often come home wanting the other person to listen and give advice or consolation. Les talks about how the child self creeps in to both their personalities during those stressful times.

It is really messy when we both are under stress at the same time. Then we usually end up fighting about trivial things that don't really matter. I pout and George will stomp off. It's like kindergarten around here at those times. We're learning to take turns talking about our days—and staying adult really helps.

Jerome and Julia have come up with their own strategies for staying adult. Says Julia:

It's taken a few years, but now when one of us is feeling down, or hurt, or little, the other one tries to stay adult and just listens until the feelings subside.

Jerome adds to this thought:

I think we are also both better at nurturing our own wounds, talking to our friends, or going for a walk or run when we are initially hurt. Then we come back and talk later when we feel able to talk more calmly. Sometimes, by then, the feelings have gone away. If not, we quickly clear the air.

As you can see from these couples, the wounded child state is not safe for either person in an adult relationship unless one of you stays adult. So what do we do with these hurt, old, wounded child feelings?

According to TA, we need to become our own best caregiver.

> You are the adult who now needs to nurture your own inner child. Looking to your partner for "parenting" will lead to inequality and imbalance in your relationship.

Our adult self needs to take responsibility for our child self. We need to let the adult part listen to this child, or take our self out to play and give it attention when our feelings have been wounded and the hurt is not resolved. If your adult self does not protect and care for the little child inside you, it is like having a two-year-old in your care and walking away when she is hurting. Or, it's like whopping the little two-year-old guy upside the head with a two-by-four, if you let the critical parent take over! It is important that you learn to care for your inner child from a loving adult place so you don't inappropriately lay this burden on your mate. For example:

- Your adult self knows the old pitfalls you may fall back into when you visit the family you grew up in. The adult self can visit your extended family and leave your child self at home—safe and protected.

- The adult self knows how to get through a difficult or heated discussion when your child self feels afraid or acquiesces out of fear or uncertainty.

- The adult self knows how to stand up for you in an assertive way when someone is bullying you.

- While your child self may not know how to say "no," your adult self can do so when appropriate.

- Your adult self can take your child self out for ice cream or comfort you when you need a good cry.

- The adult self knows how to have good, intimate sex. The adult self also knows not to engage in sex if you are feeling little, hurt, or needy.

- Your adult self can remind your child self that making mistakes is part of learning, that there's nothing to be ashamed of, and that you'll be able to do better next time.

Such tasks are much too big for a three- or four-year-old. But they are not too big for an adult.

E X E R C I S E S

In the following exercises you will begin to identify your parent, child, and adult selves. Becoming acquainted with your responses will help you to stay positive with your partner and strengthen the adult/adult interactions between you.

Take your time and do these exercises thoroughly on your own. Later you will come together to share your discoveries.

Remember that each of these selves may be outwardly expressed in your actions, or they may be attitudes or feelings that another person senses, even if you do nothing outwardly. If any of these selves or your responses to them are not readily apparent to you, simply allow the concepts in the chapter to accompany you as you go through your week. You will gradually begin to recognize these selves in your inter-actions and internal responses.

Once you become fully aware of your three selves, change will come more easily. The main task is to ask yourself, "Am I using these selves wisely? Do I revert to the critical parent or the wounded child when I am under stress? How does this affect my interactions, and especially my partnership? Does my adult self need some muscle build-ing? Which characteristics of my adult self do I need to work on?"

Since you will be identifying both positive and negative character-istics in yourself and your partner, try to remain nonjudgmental, yet truthful.

Positive and Negative Parent Selves

These exercises will help you identify the times in your life when you think or behave as the positive or negative parent—or when you feel your partner, or others, are behaving in this way.

Draw a "parent circle" with a plus and minus sign representing both the nurturing and critical aspects of parenting. First make a list of the times when you find yourself being the positive, or nurturing, parent self. Make a list of the actions and characteristics that let you know you are being your positive parent self. Identify times you experience this with your partner. Ask yourself if you are expressing the positive parent self appropriately. When might it be inappropriate to express this self with your partner—and how does this impact your relationship?

Identify what you say and do when you are your negative parent self. When do you revert to the negative parent self, and how does this impact your relationship? How does your partner respond when you are being a critical parent? Ask yourself, "When I've used critical parent words and actions with my partner, what dynamic does it produce? Is this the result I want?"

Now look at times when your partner has pointed a critical parent finger at you, either verbally or nonverbally. When does this typically happen in your relationship? How does this make you feel? How do you respond? Do you remain calm? Do you feel little and sad? Do you get angry and rebellious? How does this impact your relationship?

Sometimes we are our own worst critical parent. Explore when you are critical, shaming, blaming, angry, or judging with yourself. Ask yourself, "How do I feel when I am being the critical parent and pointing a finger at myself?"

Take some time to identify all the triggers or stressors that seemingly cause you to revert to either inward or outward shaming, blaming, angry, or critical behavior toward your partner. Again, ask yourself, "Is this the result I want?"

Joyful and Wounded Child Selves

These exercises will help you identify the times in your life when you think or act like the joyful or wounded child—or when you feel your partner, or others, are acting this way.

Draw a "child circle" with a plus and minus sign representing the joyful and wounded aspects of childhood. Focus first on your joyful child experience. Ask yourself, "How does my joyful child self act when I feel safe? How do I play, and express humor, laughter, mischievousness, and joy? How often do my partner and I interact and play as child selves? Is this often enough?"

Now, focusing on the wounded child, ask yourself, "How did I react when I was hurt as a child (before the age of eight or nine years)?" Think about your initial response. You may have had a secondary response within minutes, but it is the first response that is most important. Explore what you did "on the outside." Did you kick, scream, cry, look blank or impassive, run to your room, cry, or hide?

Next, consider what you were thinking and feeling "on the inside." You may have felt sad, hurt and confused, angry, or even enraged. In either case, what were you telling yourself? Was it, "I'm such an awful stupid person!" or "It's so unfair. They are wrong or stupid to treat me this way!"

As you contemplate your childhood responses, think about how you might subtly replicate them today when you feel hurt, shamed, blamed, or punished, or when someone is angry or misunderstanding you. You'll probably discover your wounded child responses hiding out in adult clothing. Write about how these responses impact your relationship. When you act from your wounded child self, do you get the results you want with your partner?

Your Adult Self

These exercises are meant to help you identify your current adult strengths and to explore ways to expand on them, so you and your partner interact from your adult selves most of the time.

First, take a blank page and write these words at the top: "What I notice about my adult self." Then slowly think over all of your relationships. Think about how you behave with your coworkers, friends, parents, siblings, and your partner. Make a list of six of these people, including your partner. Under each person's name, identify the adult qualities you show around this person by listing these qualities under each name.

Then, stop and reflect on these six lists. When is it most difficult to stay adult around each of these people? Make another list of an additional three adult characteristics or qualities you would like to increase in each of these relationships. Notice if the lists for your partner are similar or different than those of the other people in your life. Ask yourself: "Am I bringing my adult self equally to all my relationships, or is it more challenging to do this with my partner?"

Also ask yourself, "Do I bypass my adult self and instead become the critical parent? Do I then beat myself up, become the wounded child, feel hurt or angry, and then beat myself up again? When do I do this? Under what circumstances do I bypass my adult self?" The pattern might seem a little like a boomerang.

As a way of expanding your adult behavioral repertoire, think about the people around you. Who consistently acts in ways you admire and want to emulate? Look for a variety of people at work, among your friends, your neighborhood or faith community, and among celebrities. You may even think back to positive role models you had as a youngster, in high school, or in college.

In addition, you may list all the current professionals—advisors, coaches, teachers, and mentors—who could help you develop adult "muscles."

Again, taking a blank page and contemplating everything you have learned about your parent, child, and adult selves, answer the following question:

What do I need to do to strengthen my adult self?

Then, highlight four or five things you can do to help yourself to stay adult or expand your adult repertoire. Make specific notes and agreements with yourself about what you intend to do to strengthen your adult self in the coming weeks.

Notes and Agreements on Expanding Your Adult Self

Once a day for the next few weeks, spend ten minutes visualizing yourself acting and responding in these new ways. Then begin to put these behaviors into practice with your partner and expand on them throughout the remainder of this program, returning to your notes and agreements whenever necessary.

Letting Your Adult Self Care for Your Joyful and Wounded Child

As your adult self becomes strong and confident, it will be easier to care for the hurt child inside, so the child feels nurtured and is not sabotaging the relationship with your partner. The task is to become aware of how you treat yourself when you are feeling joyful or hurt, and then be able to give to yourself appropriately. Most of our child self's needs are small and doable—to be held, rocked, played with, given attention, given praise, not made to do scary things, and so on.

Ask yourself the following questions:

How do I nurture myself?

Now write down five or six ways you can nurture yourself when you feel a little down. Forms of nurturance might include a long, hot, relaxing bath; a well-prepared and delicious meal; sucking the juice out of oranges while sitting in the middle of your garden; time to read; listening to music; or a conversation with a close friend.

How do I fulfill my need to play?

This could be a romp in the yard with your dog, a jog around the lake, a pillow fight with your older sister, a trip to the movies, or creating a piece of art. Some people enjoy making ice cream or playing golf. What would satisfy your child self's needs?

As part of your self-care this week, identify what your inner child might like to do for fun or relaxation. Then, provided it is not harmful, impossible, illegal, or prohibitively expensive, do it. Care for this part of yourself by giving yourself enough time for play, rest, or creative pursuits.

Make a list of all the things you can do to care for your inner child when your feelings get hurt. What do you most need and want when you are feeling bad? How can you give this to yourself? Taking care of yourself in this way is very important, because if you don't, you will expect your partner to take care of your wounded child.

Most people find that their inner child is not very demanding. Children have very basic needs: to be cuddled, loved, listened to, held, and sometimes played with. See if your inner child and your adult self can create a strong relationship. You will feel more cared for and nurtured because you are directly in control of providing this for yourself, and can do so at any time. In addition, your adult self will be available to relate to your partner more often, without interferences of hurt feelings coming into play.

Talking with Your Partner about Your Parent, Child, and Adult Selves

Once the two of you have done this private reflecting and have thought of ways to strengthen your adult self, come together as partners. Take turns talking and listening to one another as you describe what you are learning about your own ability to stay adult, and about what stressors trigger you to revert to the critical parent and/or wounded child.

Share what you have discovered about your own childhood responses to being hurt. Talk about how you see yourself reverting to these patterns in your relationship. Describe one or two things you plan to do to stay adult with one another.

Your task as partners in this exercise is mainly to listen nonjudgmentally. You may wish to make a pact to help one another remain in your adult selves. One way to do this is to agree that anytime you catch yourself acting from a critical parent or wounded child place, you quickly say, "Oops, there I go again (being critical or being mopey). Let me stop and start over." As the partner, you'd quickly agree and move on.

· ·

Talk Is Much More Than Words

Talking + listening = loving

I am continually surprised by the vast differences in the amount of time couples spend talking to one another. I have counseled couples who tell me they have so little relationship time that they barely see one another during the week. Taking an extra five minutes a day to converse is perceived as stressful to them, like an added burden. Other couples say they talk frequently throughout the day—maybe phoning three or four times from the office, chatting as they organize their day in the morning and again at lunchtime—and then spend time together or with their family in the evening. I have also seen couples where both people have offices at home, giving them continuous opportunity for interaction.

In my observation, I have noted that the amount of time partners talk—the actual number of minutes or hours—does not always translate into the quality of conversation or liveliness of the interchange. Even when couples chat a lot during the day about mundane things—evening planning, Suzy's snuffly nose, the boss announcing changes at the office—it does not mean that they are discussing anything deeply meaningful to either of them. They aren't communicating their desires, longings, dreams, loneliness, stress, or need for attention.

At rock bottom, developing a consistent thread of communication is important for the basic nurturance of your partnership. It also fosters an environment in which to share your passions and dreams.

HOW MANY MINUTES A DAY DO YOU REALLY TALK TO ONE ANOTHER?

Mohammed and Sari are busy professionals with erratic schedules. They have been married for nearly seven years and have an energetic preschool son whom they take turns caring for with some help from a nanny a few times each week. When they first approached me to help their troubled relationship, they were frustrated with one another, angry and resentful that their needs were not being met. In their first session with me, they turned their bodies away from one another, had almost no eye contact with each other, and showed no physical affection. They talked resentfully about one another as though the other person was not even in the room. Sari retreated into silence easily. Mohammed's talk frequently became heated and verbose.

When prompted, they spoke of the early days of their relationship—pre-childrearing, pre-first house with many remodeling needs—

when they had stimulating conversations about a vast array of subjects. They loved to travel and indulged this passion often. They explored friendships with interesting compatriots who shared their interests in the world, art, and culture. They were wistful about these times.

When I asked them how much time they spent talking each day, they quickly said it was sporadic—dependent upon their work schedules, which sometimes conflicted. When I asked them what they talked about and how these conversations proceeded, they reported that discussions were "about more superficial things, often smooth, and even had some humor and playfulness," or they "easily deteriorated into disagreement, anger, then silence for hours or days." As a rule, Mohammed and Sari communicated mainly about daily to-do lists and to update one another on their son, as they passed his care back and forth between them and the nanny.

Mohammed and Sari were cranky and unhappy in this marriage that had become dissatisfying. They were wondering if they had made a mistake in marrying one another. I determined that they were in mourning, grieving the loss of their earlier days, with the companionship, rich friendships, and common interests they had obviously thrived on and shared. They had become devoted parents, but they had sacrificed their marriage.

It is common, once the initial honeymoon has waned, once two people have lived together for a few years, or once the children have come along, for a couple to spend much less time talking about truly personal and meaningful things. Stresses and demands of daily life become the major focus in many households. Husbands, wives, mothers, fathers, and children come and go with little time dedicated to truly focus on one another.

With little opportunity to share more deeply, couples stop getting to know one another. Because we are always growing and changing as individuals, it is easy to drift apart without an ongoing thread of communication. This leaves couples more vulnerable to loneliness, depression, anger, and frustration. It also leaves couples more vulnerable to seeking attention outside of the relationship.

Many people develop resentment toward their partner, rather than identify their lack of intimacy, connection, or love as a problem stemming from lack of consistent, meaningful connection. They fail to recognize this as a problem they can solve together. They forget that they used to feel connected, at least in the beginning, or they would never have gotten together. They forget that they once knew how to connect through talking and activities.

Let's return briefly to the first meeting I had with Mohammed and Sari. For some men and women, the resentments brought on by lack of consistent connection turn into passivity, depression, and withdrawal from their mate; for others, the resentment is expressed through anger, blame, and sometimes disrespectful or abusive language. This is how Sari explained their situation:

> *I used to talk and talk and tell him what I wanted and how I was feeling. I don't know what happened, but over the years, I've just given up. I don't have the energy. I don't have much feeling—about anything. I don't know what I want anymore. I don't know how to talk to him. I'm so angry and hurt. I don't know if I even love him. I don't know what I feel.*

Mohammed remarked:

> *When I ask her anything, all she says is "Oh, I don't know," or "I don't care, you go ahead" or "you decide." And then later she gets mad at me if I go ahead and make dinner or paint the bathroom, when I already asked her what she wanted to do. She claims I didn't include*

her. It really frustrates me. She doesn't even leave the front light on for me when I come home late at night. It really pisses me off. It's stupid. She acts dumb! I feel so resentful, I'm not sure this relationship is worth it. Maybe we're not meant to be together.

In the Big Picture approach to partnering, couples agree to develop a thread of consistent and meaningful communication—and begin by scheduling times to talk together regularly and take turns listening to one another.

In Big Picture partnering, couples have specific conversations focused on topics that are meaningful to each of them. This maximizes the quality of interaction, as well as the attention given to the partner and the topic. Partners are asked to spend twenty to thirty minutes at least every other day, or four times per week, taking turns talking and listening to one another. Each person gets at least ten to fifteen minutes of their partner's undivided attention.

Now, it might sound cold and calculating to maximize the quality and efficiency of communication by scheduling twenty to thirty minutes every other day just for talking to your mate. Some feel this conversation would or should happen spontaneously, "if he really loved me" or "if she really cared." For other couples, who do not give priority to conversing with each other, it seems nearly impossible to find the time for a conversation at the end of the day when they are too tired or burnt out. Such resistance is exactly why it's so important to follow this Big Picture Essential: talk together regularly, and take turns listening. You'll be amazed what a difference it will make in your relationship.

In Big Picture partnering, you both agree to schedule twenty to thirty minutes of conversation, with no interruptions, at least four times each week, or every other day. This is a time in which you sit down or take a walk together, and talk. Each of you gets to talk about something that is important and meaningful to you—not schedules, not the kids, not household errands—for half of this time. While you can have some interaction and dialogue, the object is to actively listen to your partner; to get to know your partner as they are today, in this moment; and to let your partner get to know more about you by sharing more of your desires, concerns, goals, and dreams.

In Big Picture partnering couples coaching and workshops, this is abbreviated to:

REGULAR TALKING/TAKING TURNS
Every other day or four times per week, twenty to thirty minutes, ten to fifteen minutes each

When first given this assignment, some couples are so out of practice they don't know what to talk about or how to fill the brief ten to fifteen minutes. If this happens to you the first few times, simply share your responses to the exercises at the end of each week and you will have plenty to talk about.

Sample week: November 15–22

Saturday Nov. 15	Monday Nov. 17	Wednesday Nov. 19	Friday Nov. 21
a.m. coffee	after kids go to bed	early walk before work	dinner out
✔	✔	✔	✔

Regular Talking, Taking turns
shows the weekly checkoff box you will find in the workbook
to help you remember to schedule 20–30 minutes every other day
or four times each week to take turns talking and listening to one another.

SIMPLE TALKING CREATES DRAMATIC AND ONGOING IMPROVEMENT IN PARTNERING

Even though couples vary widely in the amount of time they talk, the Big Picture plan for regular talking and listening nearly always works to quickly and dramatically improve the overall quality of the relationship. While Dr. Gottman's research, discussed in week 2, shows that a high ratio of positive to negative interactions is an essential factor in the longevity of marriages, my observations show that developing a consistent pattern of meaningful communication between any couple is the most important factor. Ongoing, meaningful talking and listening naturally promote a high degree of positive interaction.

When couples do not implement this agreement to communicate meaningfully on a consistent basis, their relationship does not improve. If they practice regular communication some of the time, their relationship improves during those times only. If a couple takes this agreement to heart and talks and listens to one another frequently and meaningfully, improvement is rapid and dramatic, and it lasts.

Couples who . . .

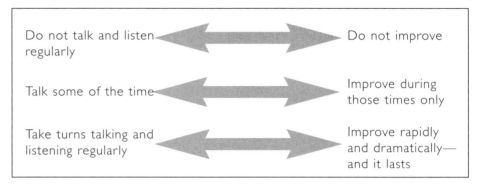

Do not talk and listen regularly	Do not improve
Talk some of the time	Improve during those times only
Take turns talking and listening regularly	Improve rapidly and dramatically—and it lasts

The high positive-to-negative ratio and a continuous thread of meaningful communication are like the chicken and the egg: On the foundation of ongoing, structured communication, positive verbalizations and interactions occur more frequently. And when a couple is actively fostering more positive interactions, they enjoy talking and listening to each other and want to talk together more frequently.

So how did implementing this essential step—talking together regularly and take turns listening—affect Mohammed and Sari?

At the end of the first coaching session, I sent them home with the "Do not fight" rule, an awareness of the positive-to-negative ratio, and the remaining 10 Essentials of Big Picture partnering. They were assigned to find regular talking and listening time and to practice talking about things that had once been important to them. I told them to do so until they returned for their next session.

Two weeks later, it was like a different couple walked into the room. They were sweet and playful with one another, reporting their progress with a bit of sparkle and humor, eye contact and touch. Talking had been difficult at first, but they were determined to see if they could learn to partner, and they had been successful in talking at least five of the eight times. As they continued to develop a pattern of consistent talking during the next month, Mohammed and Sari quickly reported more fun and flow in their lives. They were entertaining friends at a dinner party they created together, planning a bit of travel alone as a couple for their anniversary, and devoting days to play and family activities with their son. Their heavy work schedules had not changed.

During the next four months of coaching, Mohammed and Sari twice experienced what happens when they stop regular talking and listening to one another. Once the family was sick for two consecutive weeks, and they were lazy about talking meaningfully even though all three were home in bed from time to time. Another time, Mohammed brought his unhappiness about work into his marriage, and he stopped talking to Sari about what was going on inside. Both times, Mohammed and Sari slipped back into old behaviors and discontentment. After the second time this happened, they got it. "We haven't been talking enough!"

Once they fully grasped the "key" they each held to improving their relationship, Mohammed and Sari felt empowered. Together they could easily go from unhappiness to contentment—and even joy—in a matter of minutes, by simply devoting the time to talking meaningfully with one another.

You and your partner can feel empowered, too, as you continue to table your fights, continue to create more positive feelings between you, and talk together regularly and take turns listening.

The act of listening to your partner, and being listened to, validates your existence and the importance of your partnership. It makes you feel "known" and cared about. It is the thread of communication that some call a feeling of connection. It sustains and nourishes the opportunity for intimacy. In a busy, hectic, and often demanding world, it is nice to truly know your partner deeply, and to have them know you.

EXERCISES

Reflections on Your Current Communication

Reflect for a moment on the amount you and your partner talk to one another each day. How much time is actually focused on the two of you rather than the kids, friends, family, or scheduling the next day's activities? How often do you share something important? Or take the time to turn off the phone and really listen to one another, uninterrupted?

How do you feel about your pattern of communication? How has it changed over the years and what do you think has brought about those changes?

Now, think for another moment. When would be a good time to spend twenty to thirty minutes alone, together? Would it be early or late in the day? Over morning coffee or during an evening walk? After the kids are in bed at night? Will you both be wide awake? Could you possibly do this every other day, or four times each week? Do you think it might be difficult to know what to say if you don't talk very much? Might you actually enjoy it?

Develop a Thread of Meaningful Communication

Your joint assignment this week is to incorporate regular talking into your daily lives. Use the guidelines on the two following pages to help you. Some of you may find this is very easy; others may find it very challenging.

No one is perfect. Some days or weeks will be better than others. What is important is that you get started developing a communication pattern with a great deal of consistency.

REGULAR TALKING/TAKING TURNS

Schedule twenty to thirty minutes every other day, four times per week, as times to talk together. Eventually, these will get scheduled at your weekly partnership meetings, which we'll talk about in week 16.

Allow no interruptions. Agree not to answer the doorbell or the telephone if it rings. Make sure children are either asleep, being cared for by someone else, or, if they're older, instructed not to interrupt you.

If an emergency arises, reschedule your talking time with your partner ASAP.

If for some reason your partner stands you up, take the time anyway. Use it for your own reflection, perhaps writing in your journal about the topic you had chosen to talk about. You can then share this with your partner later.

Each person gets ten to fifteen minutes to talk. It is okay to respond a bit or ask questions now and then; however, a guiding principle is to mostly listen to your partner.

Take turns beginning the conversation. When it is your turn to talk, choose a topic that is important to you.

Try to avoid both safe topics (like scheduling and the children) or heated topics that may lead to bigger arguments or longer discussions. This time is meant to tell your partner about your thoughts, experiences, dreams, daydreams.

It is not important whether you agree or disagree. What is important is to be together, to be willing to share, to open up a little, to be heard, and to do so on a regular basis.

Try to begin to establish some consistency early on. Don't become discouraged if it takes a few weeks to find your rhythm and establish this regular talking time.

This week, you can use one regular talking time to share your thoughts about the previous exercise, Reflections on Your Current Communication, and to plan a schedule of regular talking for the rest of the week.

Remember to take time to talk at least every other day for the next week or two. As you work this into your schedules, you'll begin to notice a continuous thread of communication. Talking with your partner respectfully and often offers an opportunity to both listen and be heard. It will keep you up to date on one another's big and little thoughts so you don't feel out of touch or disconnected.

. . . .

Your Wildest Dream of Love

Discovering your depth
of commitment to one another

There are two essentials that crystallize your Big Picture and make it rock solid.

These two essentials, commitment to your relationship and consciously choosing the Big Picture style, will "gird" your relationship and prepare you for action. They will equip and invest your relationship with power and strength.

In weeks 5 and 6, you will explore these two Big Picture Essentials that support and fortify your relationship.

WHAT IS COMMITMENT IN BIG PICTURE PARTNERING?

A commitment is a pledge, promise, oath, vow, or agreement given in trust. In a relationship, it is typically a promise of loyalty, fidelity, faithfulness, compassion, and companionship. Commitment to a relationship before marriage or without a ceremony is a private affirmation of the love, the harmony, the bond, the understanding, and the desire two people have to build a relationship together. When marriage is entered into, the commitment becomes a public vow, a promise made in the presence of family and friends, sanctioned by God or the state, to create a life together "til death do us part."

If we look at the divorce rate as well as the number of cohabitants who break up, it is apparent that neither a personal nor a public declaration of commitment is enough to hold many relationships together. Almost 50 percent of marriages end in divorce, and 56 percent of cohabitants eventually separate.

Long-term relationships require steady nurturance and attention, continuous affirmation and commitment. It is joyful to be committed during the honeymoon and the smooth times of a relationship. However, in any long-term relationship our commitment is challenged at various times. It may be challenged by an event as disruptive and painful as an affair, by boredom, or by the pressures of children or two careers. Factors such as financial stress, moving, poor health, demanding schedules, or even in-laws and extended family may also challenge your commitment to your relationship.

Most importantly, building a rock-solid and satisfying Big Picture partnership means that you commit—and sometimes recommit—not only to one another, but to the Big Picture: an evolving long-term relationship that the two of you create over the years.

IN CHOOSING BIG PICTURE PARTNERING:

You acknowledge that you are not born with innate information on how to create a long-term relationship. You acknowledge that good and solid relationships don't just happen; they are created by two conscious individuals who decide to become emotionally and behaviorally intelligent about their long-term commitment.

This important task of developing and sustaining your partnership requires you to have a rock-solid commitment to one another and to your relationship. In addition, within Big Picture partnering, this commitment represents a dedication to:

• Ongoing learning—about one another, about positive communications, and about relationship.

• Becoming creative, both individually and together, with a willingness to share the journey and creatively forge your adventure.

• Surrounding yourselves with support—by using other healthy couples as role models, and being with family, friends, coworkers, neighbors, educators, and, if needed, therapists or professionals who are pro-relationship and pro-commitment.

The Big Picture partnering approach gives you the basic skills to handle the day-to-day details in a relationship—the "little picture"—as well as the ability to focus on your combined desires, passions, and dreams—your Big Picture. That Big Picture represents the deep satisfaction that comes from building a rock-solid and creative relationship in which your individual and mutual needs and dreams are addressed. As Big Picture partners, you are engaged in building a true home, a safe harbor for you as an individual, for the two of you, and for your family. Nothing in life is more satisfying.

NAVIGATING CHANGE AND COMMITMENT TOGETHER

One of the delights of life is that we change. People change because they grow and naturally evolve through the appropriate developmental stages of their teens, twenties, thirties, forties and, for some, all the way through their nineties. The following couples are each experiencing changes within their relationships.

Jorge, twenty-three and married six months, is headed into law school this fall. Martina, his twenty-two-year-old bride, notes how much he is changing, almost overnight.

> *He's given up going out and drinking with the boys on weekends. He's much more concerned about getting our new house and finances in order so he can study this fall. He's even treating me differently—mainly for the better. I like the changes, but my head is spinning. He's not the happy-go-lucky guy I met two years ago. He's talking to me like a real adult all of a sudden—sharing his plans and dreams about school and his future. He keeps asking me how I feel about every-*

thing, and what I need while he's studying so hard. I guess I'd better start figuring this out so we can work together on it, instead of just feeling nervous, or left out.

Retirement is another big change. Beth is concerned about her fifty-nine-year-old husband, Marvin.

He's getting near retirement, and his company may even offer him early severance just to ease their work force. I think he's afraid and doesn't know what he's going to do. He's become quiet and withdrawn these last six months. We try to talk about it, but it's difficult. One hopeful thing—he said he was thinking of taking some carpentry at the vo-tech starting in a month. He's always been a great carpenter, and we both know plenty of people who need handyman services. He deserves to slow down and do something he'd really enjoy. And, I'd love for us to get an RV!

Liz, widowed for twelve years, is a sparkly seventy-nine-year-old with lovely white hair. She loves to ballroom dance and has become deeply involved with Herbert, eight years her junior and also widowed. They talked about marriage, and Liz is considering the changes she'll be facing.

You know, when I was younger I would have been much more cautious. But one never knows how much time they've got left. My attraction to Herbert is very different than with my husband. But then, we raised a family, grew a business, and made a full life, until Sam died of a heart attack at sixty-eight—so young. It took me almost five years to get my life reoriented, and now I have. Dancing has been great exercise, a social outlet, and then there is Herbert! So many men my age are "old," and I'm not! He's able to keep up with me. I think he's a keeper!

Liz and Herbert look at each other fondly—then Herbert speaks up.

I think she's a keeper, too. We have such a good time together. We could just both go on living alone and doing our separate lives, but we think it might be more fun to do the next phase together! I think her kids and mine are having an eye-opening experience as they see us so happy, but they are becoming quite supportive.

Liz pipes in cheerfully,

I know my eldest son just says "Mom, if he makes you happy, and you sure seem to be, it's your life. Go for it!" Now that's support. Not that he really gets to have a say about it anyway!

Like people, relationships need to change. Both internal factors and external circumstances cause changes in an individual or relationship. Often relationships change because of the developmental tasks the couple is carrying out during a particular stage of their lives. Ellen, thirty-four, is less concerned about her deeply engaging career these days. She and Mike, married five years, are trying to get pregnant. They'd like to have two children before she turns forty. Here's what Mike is thinking about now.

Now that my career is finally stabilized and I'm making a good income, we figure we'd better get going on the baby thing or it may be too late. I had a hard time thinking about it until I landed this good job and finally felt successful—like all men are supposed to. I know it's kind of stupid in this liberal day and age, but feeling successful as a man is still important. We both enjoy our careers, but Ellen feels she can always re-enter the work force full time later on. Women in their forties and fifties—and even sixties—are having blossoming careers in this day and age! Especially now that everyone is living so long.

Ellen adds,

And men are more likely to want to work in the garden or play with the grandchildren when they get older. I'm actually looking forward to that time. But first, I guess we have to have the babies!

Some change is thrust upon us. Peg and Jim, married fourteen years, with two preadolescent, sports-minded sons, suddenly are taking care of two generations: their children and Peg's parents, who are in their eighties and failing.

Dad's Alzheimer's has become so much worse that Mom can't care for him anymore. She's getting tired, so we have recently found a home that will accommodate both their needs—Dad's in the apartment with twenty-four-hour care, and Mom's in her own apartment nearby. We are trying to take turns visiting at least three to four times a week. It's a handful with the boys' baseball, hockey, and other activities.

Jim adds,

Yeah, sometimes we feel a bit squeezed in the middle, but I don't think we'd choose to do it any other way. We just have to make sure we have time for one another, or our relationship will suffer.

And sometimes we purposely create change because we need or want to, as Marvin explained to me privately, when his wife, Beth, was out of the room.

Yes, I am really more anxious than I ever thought I'd be. Beth couldn't be more supportive, but it is hard to talk about—it's the next thirty years of my life—our life together! I've always been a go-to-work, live-by-the-structure kinda guy. Beth is much more easy going. She's look-ing forward to more travel, going to lunch or a movie in the afternoon, or just hanging out with me. I'm a lucky guy that way—she still loves me after all these years. I'm actually thinking we may need to join a group of other people going through this same life change. Gosh, I have always been too proud to join a group, but through work they give you some outplacement services, and there is a group for retiring people and their spouses. Led by a life coach, I think, and maybe that would help both of us get through this better. I'd like to think the next thirty years could be fun, especially after working for the last forty!

Sometimes change is exciting, and sometimes it is scary because of the unknown. Change often brings the unexpected. On the other hand, without change, we are either dead or lifeless. A strong commitment to one another and to your relationship—and a conscious recommitment whenever you are going through a major change—will help the two of you trust one another and the rock-solid stability of your partnering. Commitment prepares and equips you for the dreams and fun things you can create, as well as for the challenges that life is sure to bring.

> In Big Picture partnering, ongoing and conscious commitment prepares you for action and invests your relationship with power and strength—because you are facing the change together. You can count on one another and your partnering no matter what happens.

COMMITMENT THROUGH THE MANY PHASES OF RELATING

Any enduring, intimate relationship needs to evolve over time to keep it vital and fresh. For all couples, each new phase can be like a new "relationship within a relationship": the joys of courtship, the early stages of a relationship when we say "I think I want to be only with you," the engagement and the marriage or ceremony, the first time you move in together, the honeymoon stage, the raising of young children, supporting one another's budding careers or creative aspirations, the middle family years and work life, the empty nest, grandparenthood, retirement or a career change, the need to seek new forms of fulfillment and creativity at mid-life and beyond. These are all potential phases of any relationship. Each choice or developmental phase poses a challenge to your commitment to each other and to your relationship.

Some years ago, National Public Television did a series of interviews with couples who had been together for forty, fifty, sixty years. In this documentary, each couple related the trials and delights of their long marriage. They talked about their various stages, events, and memories. Some were humorous and playful as they spoke. Others poignantly revealed touches of old pain. One couple almost grudgingly talked of staying together out of convenience and necessity. Others revealed a rich companionship, friendship, and appreciation— a deep and enduring love—that had grown out of the life they had created together.

In this documentary, all of the couples had married and committed at a time when commitment was a strong societal value and expectation. Most of them did not question their commitment, and if they did it was not until they were much older and divorce was more prevalent. When these couples were young, there were fewer choices, and most people expected to marry and to raise children. Commitment and marriage provided security in which to raise a family. Couples came together not only for love, but also for survival. They wanted happiness, but they did not always expect this as the primary value or priority. Those married prior to the 1960s generally had a long-term vision of being together for many, many years. They did not "cry divorce" if they struggled for a period of time. A commitment was forever. Divorce was almost nonexistent. Economic stability and the raising of good and healthy children were of primary importance.

We all recognize that the motivations for marriage, or for any romantic commitment, are now much more varied. Happiness, compatibility, and the fulfilling of mutual wants and desires are high on the list of expectations. In fact, these are often more important to today's couples than raising a family or coming together to create economic security. So when these factors—happiness, compatibility, or fulfillment of mutual wants and desires—are unfulfilled due to challenges of long-term relating and everyday life, commitment to the relationship is often challenged as well. If people aren't happy for a time, for any reason large or small, they often question the entire relationship.

FORMAL COMMITMENT

There are times to stop and make a formal commitment—or recommitment—to one another, to your relationship and to the Big Picture future you are building. In this week's exercises, you will both have an opportunity to reflect on and make a conscious statement or reaffirmation of your commitment. You may have already done this through an engagement, marriage or commitment ceremony, or a renewal of your vows. Even so, take the opportunity this week to make or reinforce that vow. It is a promise to yourselves and to one another.

Daily Commitment

Another way of showing your commitment is through your daily interactions.

Regularly renewing your commitment is one of the 10 Essentials of Big Picture partnering.

> Commitment is implied in every action, agreement, and communication as you build your Big Picture partnering universe, where two whole individuals work to satisfy both individual and mutual needs, desires, and goals. You will become aware of how ongoing commitment is integral to everything you do. As you practice renewing your commitment and the remaining 10 Essentials of Big Picture partnering, you will notice that your commitment is naturally reaffirmed regularly through your everyday interactions and behaviors.

LOVE IS A WORK IN PROGRESS

In the classic book *The Road Less Traveled,* M. Scott Peck writes about enduring love. Peck speaks of the mature discipline and quiet care required to make a long-term commitment thrive. In this view, love becomes an action verb. And active loving can involve the simplest of things—the I'll-make-your-bed-for-you, let-me-give-you-a-hug-when-you-are-down, and let's-make-love-even-with-our-wrinkles moments. Long-term love is an action—not just physical chemistry or a short-term feeling of falling. It can be romantic and passionate, but it is so much more than that. It is a work in progress, much like a beautiful work of art that takes months or even years to create. When a painter is laying colors on the canvas day after day, mixing her palette, scratching and rubbing the surface, and adding more layers, sometimes the canvas looks downright awful—maybe even like a mistake. But if she perseveres, the hidden tones start to shine through, the richness and depth impact the surface, the beauty and complexity evolve.

ARE YOU UNDERMINING YOUR COMMITMENT?

Commitment is a major and complex undertaking. It requires awareness of our motivations, needs, desires, and capabilities. In essence, it requires great maturity. Some people are able to embrace their relationship and all its commitments wholeheartedly. They never look back or question their personal choice. Their commitment is solid, a given.

For others, the requirements of commitment to another person and to a long-term relationship are less conscious or steadfast. Some people may not have considered all the ramifications of making such a choice, yet they find themselves in love and having made a commitment. Some people want to give up when times are tough. Others threaten to walk out to get their partner's attention. Some have worked hard to create a good relationship but get no cooperation from their partner; they decide it is time to leave.

There are four basic behaviors that frequently undermine commitment. These are:

- Making a commitment too soon in the relationship
- Abandoning oneself and consequently resenting one's partner
- "Crying wolf" by threatening to leave or divorce
- Wanting to give up before you've tried everything possible to make the relationship successful

MAKING A COMMITMENT
TOO SOON IN THE RELATIONSHIP

We have all heard stories of people who fall madly in love and decide to make a commitment to one another—to become engaged or get married—not long after their first date. In a number of these situations, the outcome is a long and happy relationship. Usually the two people are mature, know what they want in a mate, and are realistic about what it will take to create a relationship once they are committed.

Many other times, the outcome is not so positive. Sometimes this is because a couple is young. Jennifer and Jim are a case in point. As Jennifer explained:

> *Jim and I were just too young. We had no idea what marriage would require. All we knew was that we were head over heels for each other. At seventeen, you may think you are grown up, but there is so much to learn about life. Sadly to say, the marriage only lasted a year and a half. My parents were good about not saying "I told you so."*

Other times, a hasty commitment comes out of neediness. Carla remarks:

> *I was on the rebound. I thought I had healed from my first marriage which ended in a fairly amicable divorce after four years and no kids; however, I should have taken more time to soul search. I just blamed Matt for our divorce and never stopped to look at my own shortcomings. As a result, I was pretty needy for affection and someone to lean on. These qualities didn't help either of my two marriages.*

Very often people fall in love with a terrific person, but forget they are taking on an entire package of life experiences and extended family. Sometimes they may not understand the challenges that come with addictions or a history of dysfunction of any sort.

Says Dan:

> *I thought she was the perfect person for me. She was gorgeous, fun loving, and ready to party. I'd never been married and was waiting for "Mrs. Right" to knock my socks off. Well, she did, all right. I just had no idea that everything about her past, as well as her behavior with me, should have been a red flag. She was a great gal, but she had troubles with alcohol, two kids from two different fathers, and was rarely employed for more than six months. She always wanted to go to the casino for entertainment and lost a lot of money—what was I thinking! I guess it was chemistry and a certain kind of love—but not the marrying kind of love!*

It takes basic maturity, an awareness of the long-term requirements of a relationship, education about the characteristics of a good mate, and a willingness to continuously work together to create a relationship and make it last.

ABANDONING YOURSELF AND CONSEQUENTLY RESENTING YOUR PARTNER

Internal abandonment is when your body is present, but your heart or mind is not fully involved in the moment—or in the relationship. Abandonment is when you are going through the motions, saying "yes" to things without really thinking about it or without really being committed to your choices.

Sometimes people abandon themselves and their partners for short periods of time. We all experience times like these when we are overly tired or stressed, or when we have a difficult decision to make and our mind is elsewhere.

Harriet and Kammi are in their mid-forties and have been in a committed relationship for thirteen years. Harriet intermittently experiences Kammi "going away" internally.

> *I can always tell when Kammi is going through a stressful time at work. She comes home and she's like a robot. Eventually, she'll come around after a few days, and then we talk about what's happening at work. Only then do I feel like I have her full attention once again.*

Some people have a protective pattern they developed in childhood to shield themselves from getting hurt. This can cause one partner to go away internally. Gordon reports that his wife of thirty-two years would periodically go away, sometimes for weeks or even months. They had conversations and his wife went through the motions of daily life, yet she was not fully engaged in their relationship or in life.

> *Then one day, she'd just be "back." It was the most perplexing thing. We'd both know it. Later we learned that when someone or something shamed her, she withdrew. Shame was a constant part of her childhood and she had developed a protective mechanism to avoid the deep hurt it caused her. Gradually we learned how to help her stay more present and talk out the hurt instead of withdrawing.*

Some people don't take care of their physical or spiritual health. They may not exercise, or they may lack the necessary vitality to have sex or engage in social pursuits. This is another form of abandonment that impacts the individual as well as the partnership. As Kim explains:

> *Throughout our nineteen years in a committed relationship, Lee and I had always enjoyed making love—and frequently. These days he's put on weight and seems vulnerable about getting older. I still find him attractive and loveable, but he's distracted and withdrawn. He's not even interested in going out for dinner or movies as often. We're still affectionate, but sex has gone bye-bye.*

Then there are situations when a person seems to suddenly discover they have not been happy for years. This is usually dramatic and heart wrenching, especially for the partner who is abandoned. At other times, it manifests as lots of anger, misdirected at the spouse for all of their alleged shortcomings, which the other partner claims they have put up with for so many years. Usually, such a dramatic switch in a spouse's feelings and behavior is preceded by a life-altering event. This is typically an event or circumstance that the person is psychologically unprepared for, such as a death or the diagnosis of an illness. They may act out in a way that threatens their relationship rather than choose to appropriately grieve, communicate their unhappiness, or seek help.

Doreen is distraught about just such a circumstance in her nine-year marriage. The sudden change in Jeff's behavior has her questioning her own reality.

> *We've been together for eleven years, married for nine, and suddenly in this past month Jeff is telling me he's been unhappy since the day we got married. I'm stunned. He denies having an affair, although I don't know if he's attracted to someone else suddenly. I just don't know who this man is. I know we've had our arguments and disagreements over the years, but we always seemed to talk them out. Now he says he's mad about everything I do, that I'm always nagging him; that I don't want to have sex often enough, that I expect him to work hard and bring home half of the income in our relationship. I supported him while he went to graduate school for four years, and yes, his sex drive is higher than mine—but I never knew he was so unhappy. I don't think he was—was he?*

"CRYING WOLF" BY THREATENING TO LEAVE OR DIVORCE

Another way of abandoning a relationship is to create instability by threatening to leave or divorce. Even when this is said mildly or indirectly, or even when it is not meant, such threats are ominous and loom over a relationship. A basic rule of commitment is: Never threaten to leave unless you truly mean it.

Anna and Henry are examples of individuals who threatened their spouses to get their attention, a positive response, or a change of behavior and to provoke a fight to save the marriage as an indication of their spouses' love. Instead, their partners became withdrawn, wary, or felt misunderstood.

Anna and John have been married for six years. She is in her early thirties and he is pushing forty. She wanted a bigger home and to start a family. John appeared content with their very busy life of work and socializing with a group of friends. He is a strong, silent type; Anna craves more verbal and emotional connection. She explains:

> After awhile I just didn't know how to reach John. He'd simply mumble or put me off when I wanted to talk about a new house or trying to get pregnant. He is a master at avoiding. Instead of creating conflict, he tried to humor me. But I was getting furious and started to say things like, "Maybe you never wanted kids and I do. Maybe this marriage won't work after all. You lied to me about having a family." I started to yell at him frequently, and he withdrew. I really didn't want to end our marriage. His silence still bugs me, but I love so many other things about him. I just want him to talk to me. I learned through Big Picture partnering how damaging these threats can be. We finally got help and learned to talk more openly. And I discovered through our talks how afraid he was that I would really leave.

Henry is an active guy, and being a father with family obligations was challenging for him. He felt Sarah didn't divide her time well between him and their three-year-old. Instead of talking to her, he'd tell Sarah,

> *Maybe I'm just not cut out for parenthood. We never go out anymore. You seem totally content with whatever Danny needs—and I get frustrated. Maybe we're not meant to be together.*

Sarah ended up sad and frustrated with Henry's summation of their marriage. In her mind she began to prepare for the possibility that Henry might leave someday. As a result, he became more frustrated with her passivity in the relationship until it all came to a head and the truth about their feelings came out.

> *Here I thought I was trying to tell her I wanted more time with her— not to take away from our child, whom I love—but to let her know I loved lots of the things we used to do, and the joy she brings me when we are doing more things together. I guess I chose a pretty lousy way of expressing it. Sarah finally told me she was even thinking about where she and Danny could live, how she'd manage financially, while at the same time she was hoping I'd wake up to what a good thing we had going. That's when we finally got some help to communicate better. I could have lost Sarah and Danny if I had kept saying those threatening things—when all I wanted was to be closer again.*

When couples threaten to walk out of a relationship, or to divorce, they are often "crying wolf." On the other hand, it means they have thought about it. Some people are dramatic and grandiose and say such things without any intention of following through. They simply want to get their mate's attention, or a reaction. No matter what your intention, telling your partner that you want to leave the relationship damages the trust between you. A partner will register such a statement or threat in their cells and bones, even if intellectually they know you don't really mean it. It will set up a fear pattern, maybe a fight-or-flight response. The emotional walls go up because one partner has made the other feel unsafe. If one has threatened to leave, why should the other risk getting emotionally closer?

If this is happening in your relationship, stop your threats. Now. Take a look at what feelings you are really trying to express. If you want to improve your partnering skills, learn to talk about what's bothering you. Talking about your discontent in a constructive way can bring positive changes. On the other hand, when you express your unhappiness in a destructive or threatening way, you will seldom get your needs met.

WHEN ONE PARTNER WORKS HARD TO CREATE A GOOD RELATIONSHIP BUT THE OTHER DOESN'T

One study shows that when married couples are unhappy but stay together even though they don't get outside help—86 percent report greatly increased happiness and satisfaction five years later. That means that without doing anything about their reported unhappiness, the majority of couples who stay together through difficult times come out feeling positive—even happy—about their relationships five years later. The experts speculate that much of a couple's dissatisfaction may be due to circumstances—such as job stress, child rearing, health problems, care of elderly parents, disability, etc. If they stay together, such circumstances are often alleviated with time. And when couples survive difficult times and seek support during those times, they can thrive.

I always advise couples going through stressful situations to commit to working on their relationship on a daily basis—one day at a time.

Every morning, acknowledge your willingness to do the work of partnering by saying, "I am willing to do my part in partnering today." When your circumstances are difficult, in order to weather the daily ups and downs, use your sense of willingness to help you build the emotional muscles and stamina to stay in the relationship and keep moving forward. Of course, you should seek support and help. And, if you need a break, take a few hours off just for yourself. Offer your partner time off as well.

WANTING TO GIVE UP BEFORE YOU'VE TRIED EVERYTHING POSSIBLE

When couples claim that they want to break up, I ask them to first reconsider. They need to consider any regrets they might have if they do not try to sort out the problems in their relationship. Breaking up and divorce have long-lasting consequences for both the adults and the children involved.

Getting help at this point means getting relationship therapy, education, or counseling. It means learning new skills, looking at the issues, and arriving at potential new solutions. This is important for two reasons. As we get older we cannot help but accumulate more regrets. Regrets and feelings of failure are hard on the heart. For the sake of your heart and your future well-being, make sure you know for certain that you have done all you can to make the relationship work.

The second reason to get help for your relationship is for your children's sake. As adults, you and your partner will survive and rebuild your lives. Your children, no matter what their ages, will always be affected by the fact that you threatened their stability and broke up their home. They will always live with the psychological and emotional ramifications of their parents breaking apart. They are also likely to experience the inconsistency, instability, and negative economics of divorce, no matter how well they are parented by one or both of you.

IF YOU ARE CONSIDERING LEAVING YOUR PARTNER

Sometimes breakups and divorce are unavoidable. If a couple must break up or divorce, it is important that they try to separate without threats or anger. Since this can be extremely difficult in some cases, many couples seek professional help to get through this difficult process. Again, I always advise couples who are on the brink of separation to make absolutely certain that this is what they want to do. If they discuss their potential breakup with a psychologist, marriage counselor, or mediator and still decide to end their relationship, at least they will have a better understanding of "why" and less opportunity for regrets and bitterness down the road.

There are many challenges, circumstances, and phases in a long-term relationship. Some are more difficult and some more joyful than others. If we love our partners in the active way that M. Scott Peck describes, if in our calmer moments we truly want to be in a relationship, if we are mature enough to know that the day-to-day is not always easy, then commitment to the relationship—along with perseverance, creativity, and humor—can see us through the challenging times.

EXERCISES

Affirming Your Sense of Commitment

This week, I'd like each of you, on your own, to say the following affirmations out loud every day:

- I am willing to continuously choose our relationship. I'm willing to work at our relationship, even when I am tired or the going gets tough.
- I choose to be creative in our relationship. I choose to learn new ways of doing things if the old ways are not working.
- I am committed to our relationship because I value it. I know that we can make it more and more solid and exciting if we do it together.
- If we are not ready now to create a Big Picture partnership, I can get ready by doing my part.

How do these affirmations resonate inside you? If you like, rewrite them in your own words. You might also add other affirmations as well.

Say them every day this week. (You'll be saying them again daily next week.) Write them out and put them on the bathroom mirror or on your dashboard to remind you of your commitment to your relationship.

As you begin to say these affirmations every day, notice any changes in your behavior, attitudes, willingness, or feelings of being present or engaged in your relationship.

Are You Undermining Your Commitment to Your Relationship?

Take some time to reflect on everything you read this week about the subtle ways you may inadvertently or indirectly abandon your relationship. Abandonment, even subtle, can potentially undermine your commitment. Ask yourself the following questions to clarify any of the ways you may be indirectly abandoning your partner. You may think of other examples. Write in your journal or workbook.

- In what ways do I keep one foot in and, at the same time, keep one foot out?
- Am I putting other activities (chores, time with my friends, hobbies) before time with my partner?
- Do I tend to tune out and not really listen when I come home from a long day?
- Does my commitment to work overshadow my commitment to my partner and family?
- When I am tired, excited, or frustrated, do I overspend, drink too much, or stay out later than I promised?
- Am I telling my partner what I really think, or avoiding the truth because I'm afraid of hurt or angry feelings, or am I stuffing it under the rug because I feel a little lazy and hope my concerns will go away?
- If I'm not talking about a concern I have in our relationship, am I gradually withdrawing affection? Am I too tired for sex, or disinterested in time together?
- Am I hanging out with people who undermine long-term relationships and commitment?

Spend some time with these questions. They are tough. They are about the ways we erode confidence in and commitment to our relationships.

Abandoning ourselves—by not taking care of ourselves—is another way we commonly abandon our partnerships. We get worn out, stressed out. We come home too tired, too harried, too distracted to have anything to offer our most important relationships. Consider the following statement:

If I don't fully take care of me, I have abandoned me.

In what ways does this statement apply to you? How has it affected your life, your partner, and your relationship?

Sharing with Your Partner

When the two of you are ready, later this week, come together and share what you are noticing about your commitment. Take turns listening to one another.

· ·

Putting First Things First

Making your partnership a priority

In week 5 you explored the Big Picture Essential: regularly renew your commitment to one another—and to your relationship. In week 6 you will explore another essential commitment: stay committed to the Big Picture partnering style.

The reflections and exercises this week involve a very important stage in building a full and rock-solid partnership. They include a thorough and frank assessment of your values and priorities. When your values and priorities are aligned, partnering on daily details and achieving your goals comes with ease. Realizing your dreams becomes a thrill.

PARTNERING AS A HIGH VALUE AND PRIORITY

> Two people choose to build a Big Picture partnership when the relationship itself is a priority, and when they value what partnering has to offer.

There are three things that need to be congruent for two individuals to create a Big Picture partnership. These things are:

- Knowing your core values
- Identifying your priorities based on these values
- Living your daily life consistent with these values and priorities

It is both exciting and overwhelming to be a part of our culture at this point in history, when so many things constantly vie for our attention. So many people to meet, places to go, career ladders to climb, interests to cultivate, toys to buy. We face an incessant challenge to choose what is most important and to balance short-term gratification with longer-term goals. Some people claim they like to take life as it comes. Others say they want to accomplish, experience, learn, and do certain things in their lifetime, and that this would mean fulfillment, contentment, or happiness. For these people, clarifying priorities and setting goals is a must. Experience also shows that people who accomplish a lot in life write things down, set goals, and are able to articulate a focus or direction. Without the clarity of our values and priorities, we are prone to take numerous detours in life. We may constantly be distracted from what is deeply satisfying in the long run.

It is also difficult to work toward your dreams together if you do not have alignment or work toward goals together.

Cheryl's situation provides an example of how we create distractions that keep us from what's truly important. Thirty-four, a businesswoman and mother who has been married nine years, Cheryl had a shopping habit. She overspent at the department store each month, racking up credit card debt. When she and her husband, Jim, agreed to save for a bigger home for themselves and their two small children, Cheryl faced her priorities head on. She sought ways to find internal happiness rather than distracting herself with external objects. Jim and Cheryl's mutual agreement about their financial priorities, and Cheryl's decision to face her internal priorities, helped her change her behavior—from spending to saving—so that it was aligned with the couple's desire for a new home.

Cynthia's values and priorities were compromised for many years by an affair of the heart—a flirtation, an emotional intimacy—she had with a man at her office. She had many ways of justifying and rationalizing her needs. Her husband had not provided the kind of love she thought she wanted. Earlier in their marriage he had betrayed her trust by working long hours, seeming uncaring, drinking too much, and not being available when their third child was born. Cynthia felt he had taken her for granted and, even though he had made many positive changes toward becoming a better husband, when she came to me she was angry and confused about what to do.

As she faced the reality of a long history and love for her husband, as well as her desire for a loving home life and to be a more involved wife and mother, she learned to reprioritize and refocus her energies. Turning thirty-five meant taking responsibility for the choices she had made, and for the life she still desired. It meant facing the fact that siphoning energy into a casual flirtation meant she had less energy to put into her family. When she refocused her behavior, Cynthia was excited about how much more energy she had and how good she felt with her choices, and this happened almost immediately. From time to time she struggled with wanting a "distraction," but she was able to quickly see this as a lack of involvement at home. As soon as she recommitted and reinvolved herself, her mood, energy level, and passion for life rose once more.

Martin's values and priorities were also challenged by his work environment. Married for thirty-seven years, he was a highly successful attorney, ran in a professional circle, and worked in an office where men turned a blind eye when those in their ranks regularly had affairs. Family life was undermined by expensive business trips, working late at the office, or having dinner with casual female friends. Alcohol was always a part of these gatherings.

With a wife who was committed to him and two young children, Martin justified his extracurricular activities with his unexpected grief over his wife having contracted a rare and chronic illness, which had not fit his expectations of their relationship. He had not accepted or adjusted to fatherhood nor had he relinquished his bachelor way of life. He also worried that his professional life might suffer if he balked at the established carousing culture within his company. He was unhappy and anxious, and he knew something was missing in his life.

Martin faced some initial hard work in order to align his life with his core values. After much soul searching, he decided to reorganize his work life to reflect values he thought he wanted to follow at this stage of his life. He realized that he had spent enough years having the freedom and fun of a bachelor. He had chosen to marry, have children, and enter into family life. Now he wanted to learn how to fully participate in and enjoy this choice.

Enlisting the support of his parents, his wife, and a few close friends, Martin sought feedback on how to make the change within his current company. He went over his boss's head and was able to work under a new supervisor with more stable values. After he and his wife had some heart-to-heart talks, Martin discovered other things to do with his free time and recommitted time to his family.

While he had always been a man with seemingly inexhaustible energy, once he aligned his values with his day-to-day life, Martin found that the lack of anxiety and guilt resulted in even more energy. He channeled this into the things he wanted now and in his future. He grew to appreciate more deeply what he had built in his life, and he found healthier ways of letting off steam and playing. He and his wife partnered on creating a new relationship, one that supported an improvement in her health and also reflected their more mature relationship.

I speak with Martin on and off now, and he remarks about how glad he is to have committed to his current life choices. He knows he could have lost it all—his wife and family and, most of all, his deeper sense of self. Some would call it his soul.

While Cheryl was able to bring her spending habit under control fairly quickly, Cynthia and Martin had to do some long, hard soul searching to rediscover values that had long been buried. As they did so, and as they each came face to face with how their behaviors were short-term "fixes" for deeper longings, they made some hard choices. Each of them wanted their marriage and family life to work. Each of them rediscovered how much they wanted to partner. While they naturally grieved letting go of other opportunities, in assessing their true values and priorities, both Cynthia and Martin realized how much their choices impacted not only themselves individually, but also their spouses and their children. When they realized their values and priorities, their choices became clearly focused on healthy behaviors and on solidifying their partnerships. Both Cynthia and Martin gathered healthy people around them. They discontinued anything that interfered with achieving their goals of having a good home life, a healthy friendship circle, and a productive work life. Soon, each of them reported increased contentment and much more energy to give to their partners and families.

Angela's story is another example of having core values and priorities challenged by outside responsibility. Angela's prestigious company offered her a wonderful-sounding leadership role, even when she became pregnant with her first child at thirty-three. Both her husband and the company management supported her in having a family and a career. Angela, her husband, coworkers, and supervisors all dealt with making appropriate plans before and during her maternity leave. They did this speculating on company needs when she returned and with the best of intentions. When she did return to work after the baby was born, the schedule was initially accommodating. Then heavy travel demands set in and a schedule that had been conceived in theory wasn't working in reality. Angela had to set her own personal limits. She had her husband's full support in staying true to her priorities and values. Through much hard work and negotiation with her superiors, Angela was able to create a different job within the same company.

Angela eventually did a beautiful job of balancing needs at home while also meeting her company's needs. She did this by taking a somewhat less prestigious yet pivotal job within the same firm in order to maintain her priorities, which included time with her young child, with her husband, and doing productive work. Because she is articulate and an asset to the company in many ways, she was able to continually help shape the company perspective to both their advantage and her own.

Another example of weighing work and family values is seen in Joe's experience. Joe is forty years old, married fourteen years, and the father of three. He is a high-performing financial analyst who had to choose between a more prestigious job and a life he was already very happy with. Joe had spent many months aligning his values with his work. He was in the enviable position of loving both his work and his home life. And then he received the offer of a plum job as president of another firm. Joe's wife was supportive of whatever decision he chose to make. They discussed the fact that both positions offered positive career benefits as well as personal contentment, even though they reflected very different paths. Upon investigating the new position further, Joe decided to turn down the offer and stay in his current position. He decided that the presidency was attractive for reasons that were not core to his overall life needs, and that his current position fully satisfied those as well as his professional and creative needs. More importantly, Joe valued the efforts he had previously made to create just the right home and work balance. He knew this would be hard to recreate and impossible to achieve in the offered position as president of another firm.

In each of these individual lives—Cheryl's, Cynthia's, Martin's, Angela's, and Joe's—a number of options presented themselves, and various paths could have been taken. While making the right choices can be confusing, when we reflect on our priorities and realign our life choices to reflect our core values, we can make decisions that create inner peace and are in sync with our Big Picture partnership.

WHOSE FAMILY VALUES?

While our society offers a myriad of exciting and wonderful options, many outside forces pose challenges to our personal relationships. Although politicians and others may pay lip service to family values, our culture doesn't have a very deep respect for the type of relationship reflected in Big Picture partnering. Religious affiliation and a healthy extended family may support the strengthening of relationships, but support from the outside world is hit-and-miss at best. When you walk out the front door of your home, there are many mixed messages about what you should consider a priority.

Now, I'm not even talking about major temptations here, although many opportunities to stray from a relationship certainly exist. While this is a reality and should be addressed in any intimate partnership, I am referring here to the everyday socially acceptable temptations to stray from your core values. These include the temptations to:

- Spend money on bigger houses, cars, toys, vacations, or travel, and not pay attention to financial limits or future goals—because the economic system depends on it.

- Eat, drink, or exercise excessively—because so many messages to do so constantly bombard you

- Work excessively without considering the impact on your relationship and family—in order to impress the boss and other colleagues.

- Avoid too much involvement with your children—because you fear you might come off as less professional in the eyes of your colleagues or, because you are not sure your children really want your involvement.

- Put house chores or home maintenance first, rather than talking with or making love to your partner—because society leads us to believe that these things are more important.

- Put friends or extended family above your partner—again, because primary relationships are undervalued in our current culture.

All these socially acceptable, culturally approved behaviors tend to keep us from placing a priority on our relationship with our partner and our family. If we have clarity about our values, priorities, and our partnership, we easily make choices and feel effective in balancing all aspects of our life.

> Forming a strong partnering relationship, with mutual values and priorities that direct you back to what is most important, is one way to ensure that your partnership remains stable, vital, and rock-solid. A Big Picture relationship provides:
>
> - a safe relationship in which to interact, explore, learn and play.
> - a strong bond against adversity, especially in times of stress.
> - role models for your children, who will see the importance and priority you give your relationship.

While extended family, friends, bosses, and coworkers may challenge your decisions—because it may mean less time at the golf course, shopping mall, office, family, or social functions—those who truly care about you will respect, even admire and support, that you are living your lives in a way that reflects your mutual values and strengthens your relationship. And if they truly care about you, they will work to find ways to be with you that align with your time and availability.

A NOTE ON OUTSIDE SUPPORT
FOR YOUR BIG PICTURE PARTNERSHIP

When we are striving for more connection and creativity, we need to be around others who are healthy, connected, and creative. Chaotic, addictive, or otherwise unhealthy or unsupportive friends, family, and acquaintances will deter you from fully succeeding in partnering. Choose health. Choose wisely. Gravitate toward people you admire and want to emulate. Choose to be around others of like mind. It will bless your journey; it will help your partnership stay solid and flourish. If you need to spend time with unsupportive or unhealthy people—say, a family member for a holiday dinner—do so in a limited way, being sure to call on the strength of your partnership to safeguard you and your relationship. Plan how you will handle the event beforehand, and do this together. Brush off all negativity when you leave the situation so it does not come between you. Remind one another it is not about the two of you. Laurie's experience provides an example of how this issue can present a challenge.

Laurie was afraid to introduce her father and his relatives to her fiancé, Jeff. She was concerned for many reasons. She was afraid her father, who had had many affairs and abandoned her and her mother when Laurie was six years old, would cause Jeff to doubt her as the person he was marrying. She was also afraid her father might behave inappropriately. Fearful of being personally judged and rejected for having such a father, Laurie's anxiety increased as the wedding drew closer. When she finally shared her concerns with Jeff, he was able to reassure her. Then, they planned a way for the two men to meet on neutral ground. They also planned how Jeff could support Laurie as she told her father he would not be invited to the wedding ceremony itself.

A couple's need to protect and prioritize their relationship frequently arises around extended family and in-laws. In a romantic committed relationship or marriage, it is important for a couple to put their partnership first, so that others—even well-meaning family or friends—do not come between them, or cause friction between them. Mark and Megan's story offers further insight into this situation and how Big Picture partnering, with its emphasis on prioritizing your relationship, talking and listening to each other, and adhering to the other 10 Essentials, can help.

Megan and Mark spent time carefully partnering as they planned twice-yearly holiday visits to see his large family in the country, a few states away. It was important to Mark that they stay five or six days, since it was a time when his eight brothers and sister, their mates and children, all gathered at the parents' family farm where they had been raised.

Mark's large extended family talked, ate meals, walked in the woods, and played games and cards late into the night. For Mark and his siblings, this was a relaxed and comfortable time. But the first two times Megan and Mark joined his family for the holiday, they were unprepared for the tension it would create between them. They fought all the way home and for days afterward. For Megan, a city girl, being with Mark's family in the country for nearly a week was like being abandoned on a lonely planet, separated as she was from her work, family, and friends and feeling stuck with the care of their daughter while Mark hung out and gabbed with his many brothers and sister, whom Megan liked, but did not feel close to.

When Megan and Mark realized they needed to find a resolution to this unhappiness, they were able to apply the partnering skills they had learned to this family situation. Together, they came up with many viable options. One was for Megan and their four-year-old daughter to stay home and go to her own parents' for the holiday. Another was for Megan and their daughter to stay only two days, while Mark stayed longer. Another was to go only once a year to see his family for such an extended time.

Mark was willing to consider one longer visit and another shorter visit each year. Then they needed to partner on how to make long and short visits satisfying for both of them.

Deciding to put their relationship and their own immediate family first, they agreed on a whole series of actions that would meet everyone's needs. They agreed Mark would take responsibility for speaking up clearly about his and Megan's *our world* choices in front of his family, so that Megan did not have to sound like the ogre or the "outsider" in-law setting limits with his family. Then they decided that during each visit they would have one date night out, away from the large group. They would either go themselves, or go with one brother and his wife, whom they were close to. They agreed on an alternating shift of child-care so that Megan could have scheduled free time to either nap or read or go to the local antique shops one or two afternoons.

During these visits, Mark and Megan would make sure to have regular eye contact, smiles, and a hug or kiss. They developed little signals for, "Are you okay?" "Everything's fine," or "I'm almost at my limit!" They also agreed that before either of them reached their limit, they would go for one walk together each day, to stay connected.

Using these partnering agreements, which are re-upped and refined each time they prepare for a family visit, Megan, Mark, and their daughter have reported very satisfying visits, and they feel trusting in their partnership capabilities.

Megan and Mark truly apply their Big Picture partnering skills. They consider individual and couple needs, as well as the needs of their daughter and Mark's family. Then they apply the 10 Essentials to creatively make family visits enjoyable for all.

Big Picture partnering encourages all couples to use the 10 Essentials to deal with any new event that might cause stress for either partner. Such opportunities may involve meeting one another's friends, old lovers, ex-husbands, ex-wives, or children. It might come up when one of you is called upon to meet your mate's colleagues, have the boss over for dinner, or attend a large formal function together for the first time. These potentially stress-ridden events can provide opportunities to practice Big Picture partnering and save a relationship from the resentment that arises out of external pressures or expectations.

CONSCIOUSLY CHOOSING TO MAKE PARTNERING YOUR PRIORITY

In Big Picture partnering, you consciously choose to follow the 10 Essentials because they focus all your actions on creating the intimate and fulfilling relationship you desire. You agree to develop and deepen your partnering ability, knowing that there is no such thing as part-time partnering. We are Big Picture partners all of the time.

EXERCISES

This week is a turning point in your relationship. The following exercises—aligning values and priorities— will build your intention to live the Big Picture together.

Big Picture partnering supports both individual and mutual needs. Therefore, in this week's exercises, you will be assessing *your values, my values,* and *our values* to bring them all into alignment. The exercises will also feed the activities you will do during weeks 9 through 16.

Take your time. Early in the week, spend a significant amount of time with these exercises separately. Then come together where instructed midweek. You may need to come together a number of times to complete these exercises, so schedule your time accordingly.

Clarifying Your Individual Values

Your relationship values might include:
> Feeling loved for who you are
> Being able to give love to your partner
> Being best friends
> Having companionship
> Being with someone who makes you look good
> Being with someone who boosts your ego
> Feeling cherished
> Enjoying great or frequent sex
> Feeling important to your partner
> Being together, but having lots of independence
> Not having to do everything on your own
> Having someone to lean on in times of stress
> Being challenged to become the best you can be

Having a spiritual companion or soul mate
Sharing a peaceful home life
Raising happy and healthy children
Growing old together
Learning and creating together
. . . and so on

Other life values might include:

Acceptance	Accountability
Appreciation	Autonomy
Balance	Compassion
Creativity	Delivering on time
Economy	Empathy
Energy	Fairness
Faith	Honesty
Humor	Integrity
Intellectual stimulation	Joy
Learning	Listening
Love	Meaningful work
Mutuality	Openness
Passion	Play
Respect	Responsibility
Service	Trust
Vision	

If you have never deeply considered or written down your values before, you might begin this way:

Separately, reflect on all the values you hold. Make two lists: values for your partnership, and values for your individual lives and self-expression. Typically, what we value is consistent across all areas of our life—from partnering to family to work to friendship, and so on. For example, another person can quickly see what is important to you if they casually observed you for a week.

Write about these values in your journals, or talk about them with friends. Reflect on how you spend your time, and on what has been important to you over the years. Notice what has given you satisfaction, what you have been drawn to, and what has been core to your existence. These will direct you to see what you value.

Once you have explored both your partnering and personal values, refine your lists to include your top four to seven values. These top values are what you desire to be the core of your partnering interactions and life choices.

You might also do this exercise another way: brainstorm a list, much longer than the one above, which includes every value you can imagine. Then quickly put a line through the values that you know don't apply to you. Continue to whittle the list down to the four to seven most important values.

Priorities

Now let's compare the values that you have identified with how you currently prioritize your time. Sometimes values and priorities are aligned; sometimes we spend our time in ways that do not reflect our values. For example, you might say you value quiet time with your partner, but you fill your evenings and weekends with chores or social activities that do not support this. Or you may value playing together with your family, but you bring work home, and this distracts you and keeps you from participating in activities with your partner and children. See if you are aligned, or if you need to change your partnering priorities to support the relationship you truly desire.

Individually complete the following two exercises to assess your priorities and determine how you spend your time.

Looking Back

Imagine you are nearing the end of your life. Imagine what you would like to be known for. What would they say in your obituary, or in the eulogy at your farewell memorial or funeral? What do you want to have accomplished? Think for a time, and ask yourself, "If I continue to live my life the way I am now, will I be content at the end? What regrets might I have?" Make a list of what is important for you to be, to contribute, and to accomplish by the end of your life.

Make a note of the things you are accomplishing now or have accomplished. Are there areas you have not pursued and that you might regret if you don't? Think about how you spend your time. Contrast those activities with the ones you have not pursued. What are your conclusions?

How does this looking back list compare with your values list? Are they in conflict or in alignment? What would have to change for you to feel truly aligned?

How Do You Divide Your Time?

Draw a circle large enough to write in—say 5 to 7 inches in diameter, or use those in your workbook. Think about how you spend your time, on average during a typical week. Now list the categories of activities and divide the circle (like a pie) in percentages according to the time spent. Some examples might be:

Family time for play and connecting
Couple time for closeness and connecting

House maintenance
Running errands
Sleep and rest
Exercise and health
Time with friends
Time with extended family
Work
Hobbies
Relaxation alone
Watching TV

For example:

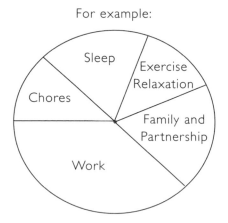

These are just suggestions. Make your own pie that reflects how you currently spend your time.

Now, returning to the list of values you created, compare your values with how you prioritize your time. Write in your journal about what you notice.

Are Your Values and Priorities Aligned?

Now make another pie to reflect how you would need to spend your time if you were to be fully aligned with what you truly value at this stage of your life.

If your values, priorities, and time spent are in alignment, congratulations! Your life choices are pretty clear. If not, don't be disheartened or discouraged. Write about what you need to change to bring your partnering values into alignment with your life activities. Consider talking with your partner, friends, support group, coach, or other professional. Discuss how to make these changes gradually but consistently so you can truly become the person and the partner you want to become.

Sharing Your Values and Priorities as Partners

Now that you have spent some time clarifying your own values and priorities, come together with your partner later in the week. In addition to your regular talking times, this week you will need another two to three hours to talk about your personal and partnering values and priorities together. If these are already in alignment, it may take you less time. If, however, you have not explored these core values and how they're reflected in your relationship, or if they are misaligned and causing friction or tension, this exercise can help you determine if you can align yourselves more closely. Without alignment of your values and priorities, Big Picture partnering is not possible.

First, take turns sharing and listening to what you each discovered about your individual values.

Now, bring your lists together. In what ways are they similar? In what ways different?

Now do the same for your partnering values.

Next, try combining your values lists. Rewrite them until they are a set of shared relationship and partnering values. Then, make a master list encompassing *your values, my values,* and *our values.* If you have or are expecting children, also add the category *family life values.*

You may need to repeat this exercise once or twice after taking some time to reevaluate your values separately. Allow yourselves the time to think through and talk about the values that fit with both of you, together.

When your master list of values is complete, under each heading—*mine, yours, ours*—you'll pick the top values for *mine* and *yours* individually and the other for *ours* and *family* together. Rank the top three to five values for each list.

Next, talk about how you actually spend your time. Are you—individually, together, and as a family—spending your time in a way that reflects these core values? Are you prioritizing your time in a way that reflects your values? Share your pie diagrams.

If your values and priorities are not aligned with how you spend your time, talk further to see how this might be changed. What are you each willing to do to align yourselves with the Big Picture you want to create?

Saying a Big Yes

Trusting the process
and each other

This week we are going to explore five principles that will help guide your interactions individually and with your partner. These guiding principles are Big Picture Essentials 5 through 9. They are:

5. Make win/win decisions together.
6. Pull your weight in the partnership, no matter what your partner is doing.
7. Make and keep clear agreements with one another.
8. Remind yourselves that partnering is a joint effort.
9. Address any problem in your relationship together— whether it's *yours, mine, or ours.*

In the Big Picture, these five principles create consistency, provide safety in times of vulnerability, and nourish ongoing interaction and growth. Sometimes they are measuring tools. They let us know if we are in balance with ourselves and in alignment with our partner. They let us know when we have broken out of the bounds of what is acceptable in our relationships. They guide our actions, make us responsible, and hold us accountable.

ESSENTIAL #5: WE AGREE TO MAKE WIN/WIN DECISIONS TOGETHER

Big Picture partnering is built on the notion that two people in a partnership should both come out winners. Big Picture partnering recognizes the creativity within each partner and empowers both partners to work together to create win/win options that will work for both of them.

This is a true partnership. When individuals compromise too much or shortchange themselves by abandoning their desires, they become resentful. Their identities and sense of self-worth are damaged.

Let's consider the Big Picture partnering universe once again. In Big Picture partnering there is no need to settle for less, because nothing goes into the partnership circle—the *our world* circle—until you both fully agree to it. Some discussions are quick and easy; others may take days, weeks, or months to arrive at mutuality and win/win decisions. In Big Picture partnering, if you are not arriving at agreement, then you may set the discussion aside for a while. Later you may revisit the topic, building on previous discussions until you have creatively and mutually honed a doable, win/win decision together.

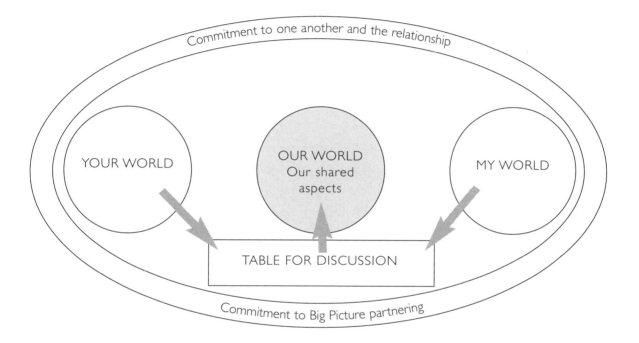

The Big Picture Partnering Universe
In the Big Picture partnering universe, each partner brings their issues, needs, and dreams to the table for discussion. Nothing goes into the *our world* circle until partners have come up with a win/win Big Picture decision.

Using Big Picture partnering, imagine bringing any everyday topic, idea, desire, or need to the table during your regular talking time. In weeks 9 through 16, you will learn a more extensive form of communicating about topics that are seemingly more difficult to resolve, where you are polarized or the arguments become too heated. During those weeks, you will learn more ways to come up with options and solutions through brainstorming and building on one another's creativity. However, the same principle of bringing your needs to the table and finding creative, win/win solutions together applies to all partnering decisions—large and small. In addition, discussion alone does not result in a solution randomly going into the *our world* circle. On the contrary, in Big Picture partnering, both partners must acknowledge agreement and have full clarity that they have arrived at a win/win decision.

Minor differences of opinion are easy to negotiate, with agreements going into the *our world* circle. For example, take Mary and Tom's dinnertime discussion:

> Mary: *"Gee, honey, where shall we eat tonight? I think I'd like fish."*
> Tom: *"Actually, I feel more like steak."*
> Mary: *"Oh, you want steak? Well, what would you think about the surf-and-turf over at Clearwater Cafe?"*

If Tom doesn't want to go to the Clearwater Cafe, he might agree to have fish at another fish restaurant, because what he has to eat isn't really that important—he's just hungry. And, he's willing to wait until tomorrow night to grill steaks at home. He may also choose the good feeling he gets by pleasing his wife.

When it comes to topics with larger consequences, it is not good to compromise or settle too quickly. In such cases, discussions that are brought to the table may stay on the table and be discussed more than once. Finances are one example of an important and often difficult issue for many partners to resolve. Richard and Katherine had many discussions, over the course of many months, before arriving at a Big Picture resolution to managing both individual and family finances. While they have been married for many years and have each brought in paychecks regularly throughout their marriage, recent lifestyle changes have altered how they handle money as partners.

Katherine's desire to return to her work as an artist, making and selling her paintings, led her to leave her job at the airline. At the same time, Richard's work as a broker of commercial properties was blossoming. He felt comfortable maintaining the family income while Katherine explored her painting. For a time this was fine. Then Katherine started to feel guilty about not bringing home a paycheck. Richard was uncomfortable having her come to him for money throughout the month. Not knowing much about their mutual family income, but seeing Richard invest in many large land deals, Katherine had a growing urge to keep some money liquid, especially in uncertain economic times. In addition to these factors, Katherine's spending style was more conservative than Richard's. Their home was well furnished, and she did not want for much, but she was rarely extravagant. Richard, on the other hand, treated his children whenever they asked, liked to entertain, bought a few toys, and liked to go on three or four fishing trips with his buddies each year.

Katherine and Richard had multilayered financial discussions as they revisited their Big Picture decisions about handling their money at this point in their lives. These discussions involved Richard educating Katherine more thoroughly about his business so she understood that his commercial deals were sensible. He also showed her where their liquidity could come from if needed. Most importantly, he reassured her of his continued interest in bringing home the necessary family finances while she developed her artwork.

At the same time, Katherine brought up the need to educate their children more thoroughly about money. She also had to face her personal fears and dislike of finances and begin to learn how to budget. Her desire to become a good businesswoman who could sell her own art was great motivation in tackling this goal.

While they did not fight about money, Katherine and Richard's story illustrates how dealing with conflict around a particular issue—in their case, finances—requires patient discussion and creativity. These are both part of Big Picture partnering, win/win decision making.

Judith and Steven's situation illustrates another type of Big Picture partnering conversation that evolved over the course of their early courtship and resulted in mutually satisfying results.

This couple has a metaphoric playing field they refer to as an ongoing part of their relationship life much like the table in the Big Picture universe. At any given time, either Steven or Judith are able to tell you which topic is currently "on the playing field." After being in their relationship for a few solid years, Steven and Judith went through a period of about six months when "We certainly love and enjoy one another, do we want to get married?" was on the field. This topic was considered individually, talked about together, and given the good counsel of family and close friends.

As "Do we want to get married?" was discussed, there was a specific time when "Absolutely! We definitely want to get married" was agreed upon and went into Judith and Steven's *our world* circle. Then the question on the playing field evolved into "When and where do we want to get married?" They discussed this for almost a year, as they lived their lives and considered their options. Eventually, a mutual decision was made. They both felt happy and peaceful knowing that the other had truly chosen to get married and be in the relationship; neither of them had settled on "yes" out of family, societal, or internal pressure.

Just as they had arrived at a win/win decision to marry, they continued to apply their partnering skills to the wedding planning process —their original wedding rings, personalized vows, and an exotic honeymoon in Bali—all of which bore their unique partnership stamp. No other couple could have created quite the same celebration. Judith and Steven did it their way by coming up with their very own win/win Big Picture decisions together.

As Big Picture partners, the two of you can put your *our world* stamp of originality and mutual agreement onto anything that comes to your table. It may take time, patience, and care to arrive at the mutual "yes!" signaling that a choice has made it to the *our world* circle. But the feeling of well-being is definitely worth waiting for.

ESSENTIAL #6: I AGREE TO PULL MY WEIGHT IN THE PARTNERSHIP, NO MATTER WHAT MY PARTNER IS DOING

> As a Big Picture partner, you have full responsibility for applying the 10 Essentials of Big Picture partnering to your relationship all of the time, even when your partner isn't.

When learning new ways to improve a relationship, it is helpful if both partners implement the necessary changes all of the time. However, from time to time we all succumb to behaviors that thwart change and prevent partnering. Let me describe a few of these behaviors, and see if you recognize them in yourselves.

I'm sure you have heard the old phrase *tit for tat*. Many couples fall into this trap of retaliating for an alleged wrongdoing, of judging the other person's behavior before considering their own, of blaming their mate and waiting for them to change. The rationale in tit-for-tat is that "They really are to blame, so I won't do anything to improve the situation until they do." Typically this leads to a stalemate, because both parties are looking for the other person to change first.

Another phrase you will recognize is, "We are only human." When we say this, the usual implication is that we know we didn't follow through on a promise or resolution, but we can't really do anything about it; after all, "we're only human." We're aware that we let others or ourselves down, but we use the excuse that everyone makes mistakes—and we fail to consider what we might do next time to prevent making the same blunder.

For some couples, such attitudes and behaviors are especially common in times of stress, transition, or learning new ways to behave. For some couples, they are daily bad habits.

As you begin practicing Big Picture partnering, be prepared for those times when you will fall off the wagon. One of you is going to have a bad day, or a tough week. Under stress, someone is going to forget to experiment with the new behaviors and approaches to partnering. It is a given. No matter how hard we try to be perfect, it is just not possible.

The best remedy for such common relationship pitfalls is described by Kathlyn and Gay Hendricks, fellow marriage educators and authors of *Conscious Loving: The Journey to Co-Commitment*. The Hendricks assign each person in the relationship 100 percent responsibility for doing his or her part. This is not a 50–50 relationship, it is a 100 percent interaction.

If we refer back to the parent/adult/child model, this means staying Adult even when your partner is letting their wounded child run amuck. It means staying adult when your partner is in their critical parent self, blaming you for something you may or may not have done.

BECOMING IMPECCABLE

Another way of thinking about pulling your weight in Big Picture partnering is continuing to do your part, no matter what anyone else is doing. I call this *impeccable behavior.* Impeccable behavior implies that you do what is correct in any given situation, even if you don't want to, or if the going gets tough, or if you are tired. It means putting the 10 Essentials of the partnership first—keeping the Big Picture in mind and minimizing day-to-day bad habits.

If your partner is under stress, you might sometimes be alone in your practice of these essentials, but hopefully not for too long, especially if both of you sincerely want a rock-solid partnership. If you find that your partner withdraws from Big Picture partnering for a long period of time, stay with the practice as much as you can. And, if needed, seek outside help to get to the bottom of the issues preventing you both from acting on your commitment to the 10 Essentials.

If, for a short period of hours or days, you are doing your part and it seems your partner has forgotten their part, remember to be compassionate. Have compassion both for yourself and your partner. The beauty of it is, when one person keeps working at the skills in a loving and non-judgmental way, typically, the other one soon comes around.

As you develop confidence in the ability of both of you to bounce back, maybe even apologize for a slip, then trust in one another and trust in the solidity of your relationship will deepen.

ESSENTIAL #7: WE AGREE TO MAKE AND KEEP CLEAR AGREEMENTS WITH ONE ANOTHER

> This guiding principle states that you are a responsible, mature individual. Therefore, you willingly do what you agree to do, within the time you said you would do it. This principle also implies that you only make agreements that are true to your Big Picture partnership and yourself. It's that simple.

In any relationship, when you follow through on your agreements, you build trust. Your friends, family, coworkers, and partner learn to count on you because you do what you say you're going to do. Some people call this "walking your talk." Typically, people who make clear agreements and act on them do so in every facet of their lives. Let's look at how Frank and Jen laid the foundation for establishing their Big Picture partnering agreements early on in their relationship.

When they first met, Frank said he would call Jen early in the following week to ask her out—and he did just that. In the early stages of their courtship, he'd call every Monday morning to ask Jen about her plans for that Friday or Saturday night. They would make a date, and he always showed up on time. Gradually, Frank started asking Jen if she would also like to get together on Tuesday evenings for dinner. This went on for a few weeks until he began to call just to talk once or twice during the week. Jen let him take the lead to see how dependable Frank would be. Eventually they agreed that they should share the calling and the initiating of plans, but they could count on Tuesdays and one weekend night as they grew to know one another better.

From this early courtship behavior, Jen learned to trust that Frank would do what he agreed to do. She learned he was a man of his word, carefully building her confidence and trust in the sincerity of his interest. They have been married for eighteen years now, and Frank is always accountable and clear in his agreements with Jen. They have had their challenges over the years, but accountability is not one of them.

Some people have difficulty living up to their agreements. They confuse their partners, friends, and associates by saying yes and then not following through on what they agreed to do. In any relationship, especially an intimate one, such lack of accountability always leads to distrust, anger, and frustration on the part of the mate, and shame, anger, and sometimes denial or avoidance on the part of the person who makes unclear agreements or fails to follow through. I am thinking about David, who, in the early stages of our couples coaching, frequently stated his intentions to engage in Big Picture partnering with his wife, Eileen. He made such statements with regard to mundane issues—like sharing the responsibility for household chores—as well as deeper ones, like attending to Eileen's need for affection and acknowledging the positive things she contributed to their marriage.

Although Eileen can trust David to follow through on his agreement to care for their son when he says he will, she cannot count on him to do the household chores or to give her a hug or otherwise express affection or appreciation. David reverts to the Roommate style of relating and unilaterally decides when he will or won't give affection. He forgets to do the chores, or he becomes too overwhelmed. Eileen cannot count on what he says he will do, and this leads to deep and ongoing strife. This couple cannot fully engage in Big Picture partnering because David consistently fails to act on many of his agreements.

Every long-term relationship entails myriad mundane and significant agreements, and it is imperative for both partners to know and be willing to honestly say what they will, won't, and cannot do. In Carl's case, he was honest enough years ago with his long-term partner, Rick, to admit that playing golf together on a regular basis was not going to happen. Rick is a terrific golfer, but Carl isn't. Rather than promising Rick that he would learn to be a better player—a promise he knew he wouldn't fulfill—Carl told Rick he'd play with him once in awhile, but that he'd rather they enjoy other activities together instead. Rick is content finding his own golfing buddies, and Carl doesn't have to worry about disappointing his partner by failing to come through on a promise he knows he can't keep. But they love going out dancing, sailing, and backpacking.

In addition to being honest about what you will and won't agree to in your relationship, each of you can become skilled at indicating a need for more time to reflect on what you are willing to agree to in any situation. For example,

> Your partner may learn to say: "I need to think about it" and "I will get back to you later this week." And they will follow through later that week.

> You will learn to say: "I don't have time to do that this week, but how about next Wednesday?" And you will follow through next Wednesday.

> You may both learn to indicate: "I never thought about that. Let me think it over, and then I'd be happy to tell you my thoughts either over dinner tomorrow night or at our weekly family meeting next Sunday." And then you will both follow through at those times.

ESSENTIAL #8: WE AGREE TO REMIND OURSELVES THAT PARTNERING IS A JOINT EFFORT

> In Big Picture partnering, the two of you are teammates, even when you are in disagreement. As Big Picture partners, you are willing to continuously work toward perceiving your partner as your teammate, not your adversary. You remember that your individuality and needs are safeguarded in the 10 Essentials of the Big Picture. Therefore, you can always consider both your personal needs and those of your relationship without being afraid that you will lose out.

There is an intricate balance in the intermingling of individual and partnership needs. Some people take a too-rigid individualistic stance; others are wishy-washy—giving in too easily, always taking care of the other person so they will be liked, loved, or perceived as good or wanted. Sometimes we say yes or no too quickly and don't benefit from adding another point of view, another perspective, to the discussion.

We also live in a world riddled with subtle everyday polarization. It is a world of *us* versus *them*. The airwaves are infused with messages about be "bigger, better, best" and have more; the implication is that we can be and have more than someone else. This makes it difficult to remember the greater threads and commonalities that weave us together as human beings. It is easy to breathe in this air filled with "scarcity toxins" and feel that there won't be enough to go around—enough pieces of the pie, enough money, enough love, enough time, enough recognition, enough abundance to fulfill and sustain all aspects of our lives.

Under stress, we tend to think or say, "I want it my way!" It is easy to revert to feelings of scarcity when we are not filled up, when we are not nourished inside. It takes two mature people—self-aware, fully in their adult selves, fully taking care of themselves—to stay out of the tug-o'-war game that is so prevalent in relationships.

It may take more time to negotiate an agreement that considers both parties, that meets both of your needs. But it is certainly better than taking an adversarial stance, which negates Big Picture partnering.

Even on the larger playing field of international relations, when countries choose to negotiate, they lay down their arms. They can always choose to reengage in battle. Negotiation, on the other hand, is distinguished by a willingness to seek out the places we come together, rather than the places we are separate.

There are some hopeful signs of people choosing negotiation over confrontation. Scientists, educators, and lay people are teaching a different point of view, reminding us of this more humane perspective. One example is the Harvard University Negotiation Project, which is leading the way in studying and teaching negotiation skills at many levels of society. Various faculty members serve as consultants to our own political leaders, as well as to international heads around the world. The books *Getting to Yes* and *Getting Together* by the Harvard authors Roger Fisher et al., describe this thinking. Another example is the Minneapolis-based Brave New Workshop which uses improvisational theater to train members of the corporate sector to "create an environment of Yes!" On the educational front, The Friends and Waldorf Schools are teaching children new methods of dealing with conflict whereby they talk it through together in a safe way, with guidance. With training at this young age, there is hope that these children will take these skills into their adult lives and impact our world in a positive way.

It requires big thinking—Big Picture partnering thinking—to realize that if you support one another in having abundance, that is, in living, growing, and creating to your fullest potential, both of you and your partnership will benefit. It is a mind-boggling paradox to imagine that if you take really good care of yourself and focus on being fully self-expressive and generous in your life—and don't worry about "competing with" or "comparing yourself to" your neighbor or your partner—you will both flourish. But it is true.

Marianne Williamson, in *A Return to Love,* referred to this paradox:

> *Our deepest fear is not that we are inadequate. Our deepest fear is that we are powerful beyond measure. It is our light, not our darkness that most frightens us. We ask ourselves, "Who am I to be brilliant, gorgeous, talented and fabulous?" Actually, who are you not to be? . . . Your playing small doesn't serve the world. There's nothing enlightening about shrinking so that other people won't feel insecure around you. We were born to manifest the light that is within us. It is not just in some of us, it's in everyone. As we let our own light shine, we unconsciously give other people permission to do the same. As we are liberated from our own fear, our presence automatically liberates others.*

Couples who choose the Big Picture are creating an environment in which they can flourish as individuals, and, working together, they can create rich and satisfying lives. To aid the generosity and richness of this mix, it is important to remember that you are on the same team. This can be a difficult thing to do. It can be a frequent challenge to partners. You can choose to maintain this perspective and to align your behavior with this idea, this agreement—even if your partner is not.

As individuals and partners, surround yourselves with Big Picture thinkers who embrace the search for what people have in common. Seek out opportunities to read and expose yourselves to sources which support this concept. Keep your individual selves nourished, filled up, free from burnout, especially in times of stress. Take time to nourish your partnership with high positive interactions. Build the muscles of a healthy adult self. Then, when you come to a disagreement or a negotiation with your partner, it will be easier to see them as your teammate rather than your enemy, as your friend rather than your foe.

ESSENTIAL #9: WE ARE WILLING TO ADDRESS ANY PROBLEM IN OUR RELATIONSHIP TOGETHER— WHETHER IT'S *YOURS, MINE* OR *OURS*

In Big Picture partnering, anything that is a problem or issue or complaint for one person is automatically an issue for the partnership. It is an issue or problem for the partnership because you agree to meet all three categories of needs—*yours, mine,* or *ours.* All need to be attended to and balanced at all times. If it is a problem for the partnership, you agree to address it together, using the 10 Essentials and all your creativity.

Addressing issues in any relationship is more difficult when one person is content and the other is not, when one person is in pain and the other is not, when one person sees a problem and the other does not. Jane and Anna's relationship is a case in point.

Jane and Anna have intermittent eruptions in their relationship, partly due to the fact that Anna is more outgoing while Jane is more contained. Anna reverts to childlike acting-out of her anger to get attention, while Jane becomes overly calm and unresponsive. Jane thinks the relationship would be just fine, if only Anna would stop acting out. When questioned further, Anna knows she wants Jane's undivided attention a little more often. She feels that communication takes place only when Jane wants it to happen.

Then there are Brian and Suzanne. Brian also feels his relationship is just fine, but Suzanne admits to being frustrated and throwing tantrums to get Brian to talk to her about things she feels are important. She is dissatisfied with the frequency of sex. She is concerned about whether or not they should buy a bigger house and whether or not they're going to have children—she wants them; Brian is ambivalent. She also wants Brian to be more emotionally responsive and to give her undivided attention at times. Brian dismisses Suzanne's pleas for discussion to resolve these issues. He experiences their relationship as pretty good just the way it is. He's not sure he wants children, and he feels that Suzanne would need to calm down in order for him to ever consider having children with her.

To get to the root of what each of these couples calls a stalemate, we decided to use Big Picture partnering to explore the differences in satisfaction level and the degrees to which each partner felt they were getting their needs met. Both Jane and Brian said their satisfaction level was at 7 or 8 on a scale of from 1 to 10. Each of them was getting 70 to 80 percent of their needs met. That's pretty high. On the other hand, Anna and Suzanne reported satisfaction levels of 4 to 5 on the ten-point scale; met needs were only in the 50 percent range. This is quite a difference in perception of satisfaction and needs. No wonder both couples had a stalemate.

This difference in contentment regarding one or many aspects in a relationship is not uncommon. Yet many couples continue with the status quo even when one person is not fully happy. At these times, the most contented person in the relationship wields the most power if they dismiss their partner's unhappiness or concerns. When this is paired with denial of or lack of empathy for a mate's pain, or a dismissal of their partner needs as unnecessary or frivolous, then unconscious power becomes uncaring.

In any relationship, if something affects you adversely, it is eventually going to affect your partner. To safeguard against a lack of mutual happiness or contentment, Big Picture partnering makes lack of contentment a partnering issue. Jane and Brian can deny or ignore that there is a problem between them and their partners. On the other hand, they are both experiencing the unhappy consequences of their mates' dissatisfaction. Both Anna and Suzanne admit to acting out their dissatisfaction regularly, either by picking fights, crying, complaining, or criticizing their mates. If that isn't having an effect on their partners, I don't know what is.

Sometimes partners will deny there is a problem in the relationship because they feel helpless to respond to the other person's needs, or they don't know how both of them could get their needs met at the same time. This might apply to Brian and Suzanne's situation, in which one definitely wants a child and the other is ambivalent. Rather than avoiding communication about difficult or heated topics, the Big Picture approach—using all 10 Essentials—can provide safe ways to talk through and ultimately resolve difficult issues. I have seen many partners gracefully work through their seemingly irresolvable issues in that way.

If the issues are too big to deal with on your own, agree as partners to get help from a trained pastor, marriage educator, mentor, or therapist.

EXERCISES

This week, individually and together, you will reflect on your readiness to use Essentials 5 through 9:

5. Make win/win decisions together.
6. Pull your weight in the partnership, no matter what your partner is doing.
7. Make and keep clear agreements with one another.
8. Remind yourselves that partnering is a joint effort.
9. Be willing to address any problem in your relationship together—whether it's *yours, mine,* or *ours.*

Four Questions

Spend some time individually reflecting on your readiness to work toward a Big Picture using Essentials 5 through 9. Write in your journal about ways you find each of these principles easy and/or challenging. In your journal, also explore the following four questions:

1. Am I willing and committed to make win/win decisions, pull my weight, make and keep clear agreements, remind myself that partnering is a joint effort, and address any issue in our relationship together?
2. What are four specific, concrete steps I can take this week to live according to this commitment?
3. How might I sabotage or get in the way of this commitment? Give examples here.
4. What support do I need from my partner in order to keep my commitment?

Sharing Your Readiness

Share your reflections from the four questions with your partner during your regular talking time. Together you can share all five essentials during the same conversation, or you can do one per day.

Take turns deciding your answers to the four questions. Spend no more than 10 minutes on each of the five Essentials per person. One of you should simply ask the question and listen to the answer. You are to witness only—no response is allowed. Take turns doing this for one another.

Continue to do this exercise periodically as you practice Big Picture partnering.

You both will have opportunities in weeks 9 through 16 to raise your concerns and needs and talk them through using the 10 Essentials. For right now:

Spend time individually reflecting on whether or not you truly listen to your partner's concerns, satisfaction level, and needs. Do you tend to dismiss their concerns as unimportant if they are not important to you? If so, why?

Ask yourself how not addressing your partner's concerns impacts the quality of your relationship?

Reflect on your own willingness to raise concerns if they are not of concern to your partner. What do you do to get your mate's attention? Or do you sweep your needs and concerns under the rug?

Notice what happens to your feelings about your partner when you don't share your needs or concerns.

Now using your journal, explore the following four questions about making clear agreements and acting on them.

1. Am I willing and committed to address any concern or need—my own or my partner's—as a partnership concern?
2. What are four specific things I can do to consider my partner's concerns more fully? And, what are four things I can do to raise my own concerns more openly?
3. How might I sabotage or get in the way of perceiving both of our needs as partnership needs?
4. What support do I need from my partner to help me do all of these things?

Individual Concerns Are Partnership Concerns

Now, share your reflections with your partner during your regular talking time.

Take turns discussing your answers to the questions from the previous exercise. Spend no more than 10 minutes on each one per person. One of you should ask the question and listen to the answer. You are to witness only—no response is allowed. Take turns doing this for one another.

Continue to do this exercise periodically as you practice Big Picture partnering.

. . . .

Looking Back In Awe

Appreciating how far you've traveled together
and celebrating the joys to come

Week 8 is a time to pause—to appreciate and evaluate how far you have come together in building your Big Picture. Congratulations! You are halfway there.

This week you will reflect on the progress you have made together by identifying:

- What you appreciate about yourself and one another
- The resources you each bring to your Big Picture partnership
- How this contributes to your feelings of being loved

As you evaluate your progress, the Big Picture approach may be so new that you may choose to return to the lessons and exercises from earlier weeks to reinforce and deepen your skills. Appreciate your choices and one another, become aware of your mutual resources, then circle back to the beginning and keep practicing your Big Picture partnering skills. Take with you this awareness of resources and appreciation for one another as you practice weeks 1 through 7.

On the other hand, you may feel you've integrated the first seven weeks' information into your daily lives and are ready to go on to weeks 9 through 16, which address conflict resolution, values and priorities, goal setting, and becoming even more creative together. If this is true for you, this week, stop to reflect on the foundation of Big Picture partnering and the nine essentials that you have already incorporated. Make a pact to continue building on them together as you incorporate the tenth Essential in the coming weeks.

EXPRESSING APPRECIATION

Sad to say, it was obvious upon first meeting Brad and Melissa that they had been together for a long time. First I noticed the lack of eye contact and physical touch. Then I quickly became aware of how little they offered one another encouragement, feedback, or appreciation. When trying to decide whether or not to move to a new city for Brad's promotion, not only did they have a hard time working out the details and cross-checking their needs and desires, they were also quick to point out one another's flaws in the process. To Melissa, moving meant that she would have to give up a life she enjoyed, living near her family and friends, and a job as an office manager, which she'd had since her early twenties. Although she and Brad both thought that moving was the best career move for Brad, they both seemed totally unaware of the need to share their appreciation for one another's efforts during this important transition.

As they began to adopt Big Picture partnering, Brad and Melissa slowly became aware of the rich resources each of them had brought to their long-time marriage. In addition to practicing all 10 Essentials, they started to notice and share what they appreciated and loved about each other. This became a pre-bedtime ritual that left them both feeling valued and loved, especially during this time of difficult choices and change. This ritual of sharing appreciation is an easy way to create and maintain positive feelings between you.

Once Brad and Melissa had moved and settled in to their new home, we had a conference call. They let me know they were continuing to acknowledge their mutual resources and to share appreciation. It had made the transition seem so much easier, and their relationship, which had previously been stable but lackluster, now bubbled with gentle warmth. It reflected the trust, stability, and mutual appreciation they felt for one another—qualities that had drawn them together many years before. Here's what Melissa had to say:

> *While I was fearful of leaving my family and friends, this move has been really good for us. I continuously noticed Brad's unflappability when there were a million boxes around, when the movers arrived on the other end, when lists of errands piled up, and when I couldn't even find the road map to get to the post office or grocery store! Small things, but I'd melt down, and he'd be right there—choreographing the move and supporting me at the same time. I feel really loved and cared about. He did lots of comforting during those first few weeks while I cried a lot! I remembered why he was always the first one promoted up the ranks in his company as it grew. He'll be a great asset to them as*

he organizes their new office here in Atlanta. And, if he can deal with my fear of change, he can sure manage his new staff. I'm happy that he has this new opportunity to grow with the company.

Brad also reflected on his mate's strengths:

I've never been very good at social interacting in the neighborhood or at church, or knowing where to hang the artwork or how to find the local cultural events we both enjoy so much. Over the years, Melissa has always brought those talents and resources to our relationship. Without her, I'd be a bachelor hermit in a barren apartment eating out of tin cans! If we hadn't started to appreciate what we have together and say it out loud, I'm not sure we'd even be talking right now. We would have moved together because we are committed, but we probably would have been miserable and resentful.

Before they said goodbye, Melissa added,

I feel so sure of our relationship and the new home we're making here that I'm starting to look forward to getting to know this new city. Next week I'll start looking for a new job where I can interact with lots of people and bring them into our lives—since Brad says that is a resource I bring that he appreciates—and it's easy for me. I like people. I don't think we've ever felt so together. With all the Big Picture partnering tools we now use, even though change is still hard, I feel like we can make it through anything and have an adventure in the meantime!

WHAT RESOURCES DO EACH OF YOU BRING TO YOUR BIG PICTURE?

If you think back to the lessons of weeks 1 and 3—the relationship styles and nurturing your adult selves—you'll recall how I emphasized the importance of developing and bringing your whole, unique, individual self to partnering. When you do so, each of you brings lots of past experience—history, learning, talents, skills, personality style, beliefs, attitudes, philosophies, likes, dislikes, and interests. Each of you also brings networks of people and connections. These are not only your family and friends, but also workmates and business associates, neighbors and community members, extended acquaintances and contacts, friends of friends, so-and-so's husband, people you know at the gym or through sports or book club activities, and so on. Interests also count as resources. For example, you may bring an interest in anthropology, coin collecting, fine art, sports, technology, music, architecture, and the like.

All of these are your resources. When you and your partner pool and share your resources, you have so much more. You may even feel blessed and abundant, just like Brad and Melissa did as they paid more attention to how their skills complemented each other's during their major move.

In the exercises this week, spend some time listing all of the things you each bring to your Big Picture partnership. Notice how these resources have helped you through the years.

MUTUAL APPRECIATION HELPS YOU FEEL LOVED

It is easy to take one another for granted. Typically that leads to a run-of-the-mill relationship, similar to Brad and Melissa's before they started noticing each other and sharing their appreciation of one another each evening before bed. Once they began to appreciate what the other gave to their partnership, they each felt more loved—and connected.

In week 2, you learned the importance of creating and maintaining positive feelings between you. As you have practiced this in your partnership during weeks 2 through 7, you may already have started sharing your appreciation of one another. If not, this is your opportunity to begin. Remember . . .

- You may be shy about stating these things out loud.

- You may prefer to show your partner you care through your kind or attentive behaviors.

- You may have stopped noticing all the nice things—large and small— your mate does with you in mind, things that make your life easier. Like Brad, you might be living in a bare-walled room and eating Dinty Moore Beef Stew from a can if your partner didn't bring her unique talents to your relationship.

- You may expect your partner to be a mind reader, to automatically know how much you appreciate them without having to say it.

Appreciation is an important form of positive interaction to bring into any Big Picture partnership. It says, "You have been noticed, and I like what you are doing. It makes me feel good. Thanks so much!"

Especially when any kind of change or stress is involved, appreciation of your own progress, and that of your partner can give you the boost you need to keep moving forward and learning, even when it may feel difficult.

So take the opportunity this week to appreciate yourself and each other for all the progress you have made so far. And I don't mean just high-fiving each other. Take a balloon ride together. Put the boom box in the window and dance on the lawn. Split a huge piece of cake, then make love on the kitchen table. Or maybe all three.

WHAT YOU'VE LEARNED SO FAR

Let's review what you learned in weeks 1 through 7:

- Week 1 compared the four styles of relating and highlighted the 10 Essentials. All ten of these essential elements must be present to build a Big Picture partnership.

- Week 2 asked you to create and maintain positive feelings and interactions between you. Remember, the longevity of a relationship can be predicted by the ratio of positives to negatives. You also learned to put your unresolved disagreements and fights aside until you improve your communication skills. (I'll talk about unresolved issues and disagreements in weeks 9 through 16.)

- In week 3 you focused on nurturing the individuality you each bring to partnering, and developing the muscles of your adult selves. You learned to identify when you were not being adults in your relationship and how to become aware of the consequences.

- In week 4 you began to make regular time to talk and to take turns listening.

- In week 5 you clarified your need for ongoing recommitment to one another and to your relationship.

- During week 6 you assessed your willingness to build a Big Picture partnership.

- In week 7 you accepted Big Picture Essentials #5 through #9 that helped remind you of the mindful and openhearted approach you will bring to your relationship. The five Essentials are about going for win/win decisions; pulling your weight in the partnership no matter what your partner is doing; being trustworthy and accountable for all your agreements; acting as teammates rather than adversaries; and being willing to address any issue in the partnership—*yours, mine,* or *ours*—even if it isn't an issue or problem for you.

- Here in week 8 you are looking at your individual and mutual resources, assessing and appreciating the wonderful progress you have made together toward becoming more intimate partners.

EXERCISES

Evaluate How Far You've Come

Using the list of lessons from weeks 1 through 7, individually reflect on your progress. Write your reflections in your journal.

Evaluate your progress in incorporating the 10 Essentials. For example, ask yourself, "Am I really living up to this particular Essential, or do I cut corners now and again?" "Am I letting go of my need to always be right or always have my way?" "Am I doing my part to keep a positive feeling between us all the time?"

As you write, ask yourself where you need to practice more, or where you have a skill down pat and simply need to continue its use.

Evaluate Your Progress Together

After you each have completed the above evaluation, come together to share your findings.

Discuss the progress you have made, separately and together, then note the skills you each need to keep practicing.

Make agreements about what you want to improve as you go forward.

Pool Your Resources

Together, spend fifteen minutes jointly creating a list of all the resources you and your partner bring to your relationship. Think about different kinds of resources each of you brings. On a surface and material level, you may contribute "things" as resources, such as a pickup truck, base guitar, or fancy computer. At another level, each of you brings family, friends, and many other "people" resources, such as mentors or teachers, handymen, or skilled workers. At the deepest level, each of you brings lots of past experience, knowledge, interests, and characteristics. Identify these talents, skills, connections, and possessions that enhance and support your relationship.

Share Your Appreciation

Take time this week to celebrate your progress in building a rock-solid partnership. Make a nice meal together and dance in the kitchen to the music playing when you fell in love. Make popcorn. Snuggle and watch your favorite video. Play hooky from work and take in a matinee movie. Hold hands. Watch a sunset or sunrise together.

Spend some time during this celebration sharing your appreciation for your partner—and for your new or enhanced partnership. Tell your partner what they have done or said to make you feel loved.

Take special notice of the things your partner has added to their repertoire of actions and ways of communicating with you.

Sometimes good things are difficult to hear or take in. If they are for you, tell your partner,

This is what I heard you say you appreciate about me:

_____

_____.

Thanks!

PART II

Creating a Life Together

. . . .

Creativity Trumps Conflict

*Resolving problems and
differences creatively*

This week you are going to begin a process to resolve disagreements and handle "hot topics" constructively, successfully, and creatively. You are going to build on this approach throughout the next six weeks and apply it to your daily details. You know what these issues are—they include everything from household chores to scheduling a social life to parenting to . . . you name it! Then you will apply mutual creativity to your bigger dreams. Using the 10th and final Essential: resolve conflicts and create new options together through dialogue and imagination.

THE MAGIC OF DIALOGUE AND IMAGINATION

In the coming weeks, you are going to apply Big Picture methods to:

- Deal with difficult or unresolved issues that often lead to hurt, resentment, blame, and sometimes bitterness when left unresolved.

- Communicate about the daily details of your lives so you do not have to "reinvent the wheel," get into spats, or feel like you are going in different directions about everyday details.

- Become more creative together as you seek and invent new options and solutions for old problems or newly imagined dreams.

First, you are going to turn communication into resolution. This naturally unleashes energy that can become mutual creativity when you grab onto it, leading to mutual solutions. It prevents you from getting stuck on difficult problems. The key is to shift your perspectives from problem to opportunity. Dialogue and your combined creativity can become a powerhouse. You will be empowered and it will energize your relationship in new and exciting ways.

A STORY OF RESOLUTION

I had worked with Sharon and Doug on and off through various phases of their relationship. Sometimes I coached Sharon as we covered a broad terrain of issues and goals, especially her desire to sort out her career while also being a forty-something mom of a four-year-old preschooler.

Married for over twenty-five years, Doug and Sharon had created a partnership with much contentment and some compromises. Periodic coaching focused on improving their communication and clarifying their agreements. Over the years they had changed their relationship from a Roommate style with some traditional components to a solid Big Picture relationship. They had embraced the 10 Essentials and, in doing so, had created solidity in their finances, parenting, and sharing household tasks, and creating a full social life of mutual friends and activities. They also supported one another's individual needs: Doug's work life in which he officed at home but also traveled periodically and Sharon's volunteer work at their son's school. Sharon gently sought more closeness and intimacy. Although he may not have sought this on his own, Doug learned that developing a close relationship with Sharon had made him a happier person.

As I think about this couple, what stands out in my mind is one particular issue that remained unresolved for Sharon and Doug for many years. Something had happened in their relationship fifteen years prior. Over the course of our conversations, Sharon would revisit this particular incident once or twice a year. I was initially stumped at how to help her resolve the incident. I did know that this unresolved issue kept Sharon and Doug from fully enjoying closer intimacy and joy.

In some ways, Doug was unaware of the small fissure that had grown between them. However, Sharon was aware that Doug did not fully understand how he had hurt her years earlier. This made her distrustful of him. She was a bit cautious and careful with her feelings. At times, this small rift even made her feel less free in the bedroom. For her, it symbolized a place in their long relationship where Doug did not see or understand her clearly. He did not "know" her. It began with an incident in which Doug had embarrassed her and hurt her feelings in front of other people. He had not heard her correctly and he had misinterpreted her motivations. This incident harmed her trust of him. It dampened her playfulness, and she protected small parts of her heart so she would not get hurt in that way again.

If you knew the details of this incident, you might think, "It's a seemingly small incident. Why doesn't Sharon let it go? Why doesn't she just put it to rest? Doug obviously loves her, he's apologized, and they have a good partnership. Why won't she just get on with it?" Some people would have swept it under the rug. Others would have denied this little place that festered, this place that kept Sharon from feeling close to Doug both emotionally and sexually. Sharon could feel this small withholding, even if Doug was seemingly unaware of it.

I trust human intuition, the "knowing" inside of those who are in touch with something within. Sometimes we don't understand why it is speaking to us, or we may fear the outcome if we follow its call. But one thing I do know, if people are healthy, this knowing, this small voice or inkling or niggling sense or discomfort always holds a truth. This voice within is trying to tell us something, if we are willing to pay attention. In a partnership, you have two wonderful truth tellers, if you are willing to listen to them. These intuitive inner selves can tell you when you don't feel connected to someone or when something may not be good for you. They can protect you from lies or deceit, remind you to lock the door or turn off the oven, and help you to avoid a pothole so you don't sprain your ankle.

Your inner voice knows when someone has seen, heard, and witnessed you clearly. Sharon had talked about the incident with Doug, but while he had said the words "I'm sorry," resolution was not achieved. Sharon was highly sensitive to the lack of understanding behind his words. She longed to be fully understood by her husband. She was seeking this full understanding.

But nothing quite resolved it.

Then one day in my office, this incident came up again as Sharon talked about a place in their relationship that was superficial. It again dated back to the time years before. This time when she spoke about the incident, Sharon was gentle, sad, and loving, whereas previously she had been angry and demanding when she talked about the experience. And Doug was truly "present" that day. Sometimes he was awfully busy and acted like he had some place to go that was more important than being with her for a few more minutes—especially when this topic came up. On this particular day, however, even though he had the same busy schedule, he listened without avoiding Sharon's pain or taking on any blame. He saw this woman he loved dearly, and for the first time he truly understood that he had hurt her, even though he had not intended to. And he understood fully, for the first time, that this hurt had continued to impact her in many small ways for all these years. He saw that this hurtful experience had left doubts in her mind about the quality of their relationship and his true love of her.

This time, when Doug said, "I'm so sorry. I never wanted to hurt you like that and I see that I have hurt you deeply," the very air in the room changed.

For a few minutes, it was as though I was not even in the room. I was witness to a small but incredibly intimate moment in their long and loving partnership.

From that moment on, the issue totally evaporated.

While Sharon and Doug had been developing a solid partnership over those many years, within months of this conversation there was a noticeable difference in their playfulness, sensuality, and gentleness with one another. It was as though tenderness had enveloped them. They "fell back in love." Sex became passionate in a way it had not been since they were young lovers during courtship.

Another new feature in their partnering skills also became noticeable. Rather than continuing to discuss the day-to-day demands of their family life—which they accomplished well—Sharon and Doug began to talk about new projects and adventures they wanted to do together and with their young son. They expanded their social life, renovated their older home, and planned for Sharon's return to school so she could pursue a writing career. Doug even took on a business associate in his small electrical company. They started to think and behave with a zest and joy that comes when a couple feels truly connected with one another, truly accepted by one another, and truly partnered.

Just like Sharon and Doug, you and your partner can reap the benefits of Big Picture partnering and expand your ability to deal with conflict in ways that are more creative.

By implementing the 10 Essentials, you will have all the tools you need to

- Be fully listened to and fully understood
- Fully resolve conflicts so they no longer produce a chasm between you

And just like Sharon and Doug, you can experience how true conflict resolution unleashes creative energy. Unresolved or buried conflicts are like roadblocks, chasms, or detours in the flow of love between partners. Conflict that is unresolved is draining. It is a siphon, a leakage in the very life force that flows within and between you. By applying the Big Picture, you will resolve old, problematic issues between you, and you will benefit from:

- Increased emotional and physical passion
- More playfulness and tenderness
- Increased energy and desire to share mutual dreams and goals

You will do this by practicing the final Essential of Big Picture partnering: resolve conflicts and create new options together through dialogue and imagination. In weeks 9 and 10, you will be reminded of healthy communication tools and you will learn the Intentional Dialogue. You will apply these to anything unresolved in your relationship. In addition, during weeks 11 through 16, you will apply the Intentional Dialogue and other creative communication skills to your goals and dreams so you can build the life you want together.

Before we turn to the Intentional Dialogue in week 10, let's look at some basic wisdom for communicating around any topic, but especially around "hot topics" or conflicts.

COMMON COMMUNICATION WISDOM

Even before the research was completed on relationship longevity and communication styles in long-term couples, much was known about basic, good communication. If you want to practice Big Picture partnering, this common wisdom is fundamental. You are probably already using most of these guidelines. If not, refresh yourself with this list to increase your awareness and skill.

USE "I" MESSAGES WHEN SPEAKING.

"I messages" tell of your inner experience. For example, "I want to please you right now, but the kids need help with their homework. I'd like us both to help them, then we can relax once they are in bed. Would that work for you?" Let your partner tell you their inner experience and be willing to listen to it.

DON'T "MIND READ."

Mind reading is trying to figure out, or assuming that you already know, what your partner is thinking or feeling. It is telling them what they are thinking and feeling rather than listening to what they have to say.

SPEAK FOR YOURSELF.

In adult interactions it is best if each person speaks for himself or herself. It helps if you don't prejudge your partner's thoughts or feelings. Each of you has a separate inner experience, and each experience is valid. One does not negate the other. It is easier for your partner to listen to you if you "speak for yourself," plus, they are more willing to open up and talk to you if they feel safe and listened to.

BE RESPECTFUL.

Think of how you would communicate if you did so with grace and dignity, if you treated another person with grace and dignity. You would never swear at, berate, or belittle them. You wouldn't interrupt them. You would definitely not blame, shame, or criticize them. You wouldn't raise your voice. And you wouldn't tease them inappropriately, use sarcasm or do anything that had a hurtful intent.

Instead, you would choose your words carefully when delivering thoughts that might cause pain, concern, or anger. I don't mean you would "mince your words" or treat another adult like a child who can't handle feedback or critique. But rather, you would communicate with the "intention to achieve understanding" versus an "intention to harm or drive the other person away."

These are the basic ways to open the doorway to communication. Research shows that this is exactly what couples need to do if they want their relationships to last. They need to talk, feel safe in talking, and keep talking with one another, just as you have been doing these past eight weeks.

If, on the other hand, you have a different style of fighting or dealing with conflict, these basic rules of communication may not be enough for your relationship. In the next section, you will learn about different ways that couples approach disagreement. You will see how some couples are more effective in resolving their conflicts than others. Then we will discuss how you can become effective Big Picture partners in successfully resolving your own conflicts and mutually arriving at creative solutions together.

DIFFERENT APPROACHES TO CONFLICT AND WHAT WORKS

Fighting, arguing, and disagreeing are part and parcel of any long-term relationship. They are unavoidable if you get close to another human being. They are unavoidable if you live together. It's not how much you disagree or fight that is problematic, if you keep the positive interactions and feelings flowing, as you learned in week 2. In and of themselves, disagreements or arguments are not bad. The research on long-term couples, however, is conclusive about two aspects of conflict and fighting:

> Couples need a safe and mutual style for disagreements or fights, if they don't already have one, and couples need resolution to fights and disagreements. Relationships in which disagree-

ments or arguments are resolved have greater contentment and longevity.

Observation of couples shows three basic approaches to handling conflict. These are exemplified by couples who

- argue heatedly, then "kiss and make up"
- talk everything through calmly, never seeming to disagree or argue
- have two different styles of fighting or disagreeing and often end up hurt, angry, and with issues left unresolved.

If you and your partner have a similar style of handling conflict, then you will probably be more effective in resolving disagreements. If, on the other hand, you have a dissimilar way of approaching conflict, then you may experience difficulty reaching a resolution. Let's look at three examples of how couples handle conflict.

Wally and Bette have been married for over twenty-six years. They met in high school, married in their early twenties, and have successfully raised four children, who are now ages eighteen to twenty-five. While their house may be a bit on the messy side—with dogs, cats, art and work projects in every room—there is a palpable warmth, generosity of heart, and playfulness that is contagious when you are around this ebullient couple and their highly interactive family. When asked how they have managed to build such a solid relationship, Bette and Wally share what they feel is a key ingredient. Says Bette,

> *We were drawn to each other right from the start.*

Wally adds,

> *Yeah. I loved her energy, lack of self-consciousness, and ability to have a good time even when doing serious things. We're both like that.*

Bette continues laughing heartily,

That part of our relationship has been one-half of the equation. And the other half is that we fight! That's right, we fight. Good old out-and-out loud voices, lots of opinions, both having our total say—maybe nobody listening.

Wally agrees.

It's all but the kitchen sink. The kids know enough to get out of Mom and Dad's way and mind their own business. It's all but throwing pots and pans around here for a few minutes. But then it's over. Things get real quiet for a half hour or so, and then she gets real sweet to me.

Bette chuckles, taking the bait playfully.

You're right. I like a good row, but then I love to kiss and make up. He doesn't do so bad himself!

Bette and Wally exemplify the couple that fights, like cats and dogs, comes to resolution, and then kisses and makes up. If both you and your partner handle conflict this way, it might work for you most of the time. It will work if, for every fight, you also add the 5-to-1 positive-to-negative ratio, and you fight fairly or respectfully. Wally and Bette learned to do this using the 10 Essentials. As Wally explains,

When the kids were little, we fought and made up the same way, only we were more hurtful in what we said. We didn't even remember the words, but one of our eldest kids, Mickie, did, and he asked if we were going to get a divorce or something bad. We realized we had to be careful or the kids would get the wrong impression.

Bette clarified:

We didn't want them to be afraid, because we knew there was no way in h___ we were going to split up. We're just noisy people! What worked, and what we've continued to use, are the Big Picture partnering skills. I think we had three coaching sessions and it's worked ever since.

Wally and Bette then explained which Big Picture partnering skills they use to this day—and every day—to balance their loud and boisterous style of conflict. Says Wally,

I think about the rules for fighting almost every day. First, we stopped saying hurtful things and stopped swearing at one another when we were yelling.

Bette adds,

I know it sounds silly, but now when we yell and holler, we just do it respectfully!

Wally continues,

Then, we naturally kiss and make up and get back to our usual interaction—which is darn fun most of the time. If ever one of us is down, we may just give a bit more than normal and usually we bounce right back. We naturally do lots of nice things for each another and that is the key. We are stuck to one another. What we've got going is like glue. Nobody's going anywhere.

Bette says,

We explained that to Mickie and the other kids. Now they just roll their eyes and know we'll get over it whenever we start to argue. They trust that we are a family. They see us fight, but they also see lots of kissing, hugs, banter, and loving between us. They know we are solid, and so are they.

Wally adds a final note.

Yeah, the kids also have developed this style of arguing then making up—not surprising with us as parents! All of them have agreed, at one time or another, that they'd rather grow up in a lively household like ours than in a quiet home where you can't tell if people really love one another.

Let's look at another couple with a totally opposite style of dealing with conflict. You may recognize yourself as you listen to Ned and Arlyce. After meeting with them twice, I had to ask if they ever fought or disagreed. Arlyce acknowledged,

Actually, we disagree quite a lot. We have differing political views, thoughts about how people should act, and even some interesting philosophical differences about the meaning of life.

Ned agreed.

We just aren't the kind of people who get very loud or angry when we disagree. I think we both were influenced by our families. Both sets of parents really respect one another's points of view and have serious debates about religion, philosophy, politics, even the weather! It was the way we had family discussions at the dinner table almost every night.

Arlyce informed me,

We even met in college debate class. We simply discuss things, talk until we both have been listened to, and then move on. I know some couples might find it tedious to talk as much as we do, but we both enjoy lots of verbal interaction. It is intellectually stimulating and it makes the two of us feel close.

Ned concluded with a nod and a chuckle.

> *I know Arlyce really loves me because she listens to everything I have to say, and I have a lot to say! I try to do the same for her. Not many other women would be so interested in all my thoughts—magnificent or irrelevant!*

As you can see from Ned and Arlyce's story, when you both like to discuss things in a manner that never looks like an argument or disagreement, when you both are civil and avoid loud voices and harsh words, and when you both really listen to one another's points of view, this style of conflict can work.

Now let's turn to a relationship where each partner has a different way of dealing with conflict. Avril and Isaiah have been together for six years. This is how Isaiah described their different styles:

> *I love her, but I'm getting worn down. Avril is always on my case. It seems like everything becomes a big issue, and she has to talk about it. After awhile, I just tune her out. I don't want to. It wasn't like this before we moved in together. I made her happy back then, I guess.*

Avril sputtered trying to explain her side of the story to me, almost in tears, with anger brimming under her words.

> *You used to listen to me, or so I thought. Now, you walk out of the room! You won't talk to me! I get so frustrated. If only he knew that if we just talked about it we could easily clear the air and I'd be happy. I know it seems like I'm always upset with him about something—but it's because he won't talk to me! If he talked we'd get over it quickly. I just know we would.*

Isaiah retorted quietly,

I can't help it. If you'd just calm down, maybe I could think. Did it ever occur to you that I'd come talk to you? But my mind goes blank. I end up feeling stupid and belittled by you. I saw my mom treat my dad that way. It took me a long time to realize she was just as frustrated as my dad who would roll his eyes and walk away from her when she was angry. I guess maybe my mom and Avril are both hurting, but I can't stand the yelling and don't know how to get her to calm down.

Avril and Isaiah were both hurting. They had everyday issues they disagreed about and could not resolve because they could not talk about them in an effective way. On top of that, they felt alienated from one another, and angry with one another's way of dealing with conflict. The longer this went on, the more they both felt misunderstood and unloved.

The research shows that if you have differing styles of fighting or disagreeing, you probably aren't able to effectively resolve your conflicts. If this is the case for you and your partner, the two of you will need to learn a safe and mutual style for resolving conflicts.

Avril and Isaiah are a common and almost classic example of a couple in which one person appears conflict-avoidant, and the other person appears to seek engagement or conflict. When you mix these two styles of dealing with conflict, it can seem like trying to mix oil and water.

A regular complaint among couples like Avril and Isaiah is that one spouse is more verbose, explosive, or needs to talk it through "right now," while the other spouse leaves the room or grows silent like a brick wall. If the more verbally aggressive partner goes on for too long, sometimes the quiet person explodes aggressively. This can lead to more verbal assaults on the part of the aggressive partner, or it may result in the quiet partner getting the "space" they need after causing the verbal partner to go away hurt and confused by an uncharacteristic rageful outburst. Couples like this often end up in stalemate. Disagreements pile up—unresolved. If this goes on for too long, issues hang heavy around their relationship, like threatening dark clouds. And as Dr. John Gottman's research would note, these couples are more likely to break up, especially because the positive interactions often do not outweigh the negative.

Avril and Isaiah were skeptical that any kind of intervention would help their relationship, but they were anxious to try something new. Isaiah said,

> *I just don't want to throw away the last six years and then find out we could have fixed it. I know there must be things we both can learn to change.*

Avril agreed.

> *Even if we do break up or never get married, at least we'll know why. At least, that's what I'm hoping for.*

In relationships like Avril and Isaiah's, issues go unresolved for months or even years, yet the couple continues to use the same old style of arguing. When such folks want to learn how to partner, the first requirement is that they agree to stop fighting for now—just like you have been instructed to do. This gives you time to nurture the good feelings, practice regular talking, and implement the other 10 Essentials of Big Picture partnering. You want to be on the same team —more connected and intimate—so you can tackle the issues together. Otherwise, you are simply tackling and hurting one another with your blame and disappointment. On this point, I agree with John Gottman that dialogue (specifically mirroring, which you will learn in week 10) is not effective when couples are in the heat of battle. They need to be calm before they are ready to listen to one another.

When couples fight over and over about the same issues, if an issue hasn't been resolved after many days, weeks, or months, continuing to fight is surely not going to work! The "do not fight" rule is for the short term so couples can shore up positive feelings and experiences, just as you have been doing in your partnership. Typically, couples who fight a lot are so worn out and so relieved not to fight anymore that they willingly agree—with the caveat that "you will talk about the disagreements, but only when you both feel more safe and are able to communicate respectfully."

Avril and Isaiah were ready and willing to agree to the "do not fight rule." Then they spent the next few months learning how to handle conflict in a way that was new for both of them, in a way that was safe, effective, and mutually beneficial. They practiced taking time-outs when a discussion became too heated. They agreed to come back to discuss issues in a mutually calm and respectful way later. Avril learned that, given time and space, and with a gentler and less angry approach on her part, Isaiah would tell her what was on his mind. She had to slow down. Isaiah had to learn to speed up his response time a bit and risk talking to Avril.

First, Avril and Isaiah scheduled regular talking time for twenty- to thirty-minutes every other day. They practiced actively listening to one another. Gradually they used the Intentional Dialogue, which you will learn in week 10. As they practiced, major areas of conflict became mutually workable and they became more creative problem solvers. They still did not agree on everything, but then, no two people do. Instead, they engaged in understanding one another's point of view. How did they feel about making this change? Here's what Avril had to say:

It never occurred to me how much I was assuming about Isaiah's point of view—on everything! I used to listen to him and felt we were pretty similar. Now when I stop to actually listen to him again, I don't always find that we agree on something, but I do feel connected. And he's listening more to me. I feel understood. It's funny how being listened to is much more important now than having him always agree with me.

Isaiah gave Avril's hand a squeeze. He said jokingly,

I agree. We know that she's not always right! No, seriously, we are just much more respectful. I have learned not to run away from her anger. She still gets upset with me, but I can hear her now. When something bothers one of us, we ask to talk. If we can't do it then, we make a time later. At first it took a much longer time to talk things through. Now that we've cleared the air on the big things, a disagreement may take five or ten minutes to talk through.

Said Avril,

This leaves us lots more time for the pleasurable things we both enjoy. It's more like when we first met. I think we both have tapped back into the reasons we were drawn together.

Once Avril and Isaiah sorted through the bigger unresolved issues, they went on to plan a wedding, purchase a new home, and start the family they both wanted. They continue to use the 10 Essentials and especially the Intentional Dialogue when they are in conflict. They also use the other creative applications you will find in weeks 11 through 16 to develop new options and creative outcomes in their life together. Avril exclaimed,

To think that we almost broke up nine years ago! Two kids, happy jobs, and a calm home life are our reward.

Isaiah added,

I know we have the skills to continue to develop contentment in the coming phases of our life together—as the kids get older, and as we get older. It's a good feeling to be successful—not perfect, by any means— but successful, and not only at work, but also with one another and our family.

If you were fighting a lot prior to starting this Big Picture partnering approach, and if you are still in continuous conflict and have not been able to implement the Big Picture Essentials 1 through 9, I encourage you to consider seeking a good therapist, marital counselor, coach, peer mentor, or educator. Such expert guidance will help the two of you sort through your difficulties. Then you will be ready to use the 10 Essentials and create the Big Picture you desire.

On the other hand, if you are ready, let's first apply your Big Picture skills to the daily details—your everyday needs and interactions—to create a rock-solid foundation that will last the rest of your lives. Some of your daily details and goals will include issues that you typically argue or disagree about, perhaps handling the household chores or finances, the frequency of sexual intimacy, or parenting your children. Using the Big Picture approach to partnering, in weeks 10 through 16 you will learn a new way to resolve your conflicts and create mutual solutions to your daily needs.

Once your daily details are running smoothly, you will apply this same Big Picture approach to bigger goals and future dreams.

When you engage in Big Picture partnering, you learn to see conflict from a new vantage point. Conflict is transformed from a battle between enemies into an opportunity to creatively problem-solve together. Creative problem-solving is applied to your daily details until they run smoothly. On this rock-solid foundation, your mutual creativity is then expanded to your Big Picture dreams and future goals.

In Big Picture partnering, disagreements become opportunities to:

Learn about one another's unique view of a situation or choice.
This is because you have chosen to partner as two adult selves. You have agreed to go for win/win decisions, to work on the same team, and so on, using the 10 Essentials of Big Picture partnering.

Come up with new and creative options together.
This becomes possible when you implement Essential #10: resolve conflicts and create new options together through dialogue and imagination. You will use the Intentional Dialogue and your creative abilities to brainstorm, arrive at mutual goals, devise new options for action, and work together on large and small individual and partnering goals. You will learn all of this in weeks 10 through 16.

EMOTIONAL OVERLOAD AND HOW TIME-OUTS CAN BE HELPFUL

Let's refer back to Avril and Isaiah and the common scenario where one person is more verbose, maybe more explosive, and more insistent on their need for communication while the other person tends to shut down, become a brick wall, become tongue-tied or even walk out of the room when their partner is talking.

Research has found that many men go into a fight-or-flight response in the face of certain kinds of communication. Using bodily measures such as electrodes, researchers have shown that some men actually become emotionally "flooded." That is, they are not able to think. They sweat. Their hearts beat faster. They freeze or they want to run. Sometimes they fight back by verbally exploding in order to push the threatening situation or person away. While the researchers did not hook women up to electrodes, I have noted this same fight-or-flight reaction in some women whose mates are more verbally aggressive and insistent. Melody, for example, reported the following:

> *I don't want to shut down, but Arnie's such a big guy, he has such big energy, and when he is upset about something he just talks and talks—at me. I get confused. I feel like he's right about some things, but I just can't think. I can't even respond, and that makes him even more upset. I end up physically drained and sometimes kind of depressed.*

Let's make something very clear here. Both Avril and Arnie need to know, and maybe you need to know, that if your partner shuts down it is not by choice. Rather, it is their body's instinctual response, a remnant from the times when we needed to physically flee from or fight threats to our very existence! It is pretty darn difficult to have effective communication, to get a positive response, if you or your mate is feeling threatened and in fight-or-flight mode. In addition, the fact that you or your partner goes into fight-or-flight is no one's fault. On the other hand, if you are the more verbose, excitable, verbally insistent or aggressive partner, you will not get what you want—you will not get your needs met—if you continue to use this approach with this particular type of mate.

And, if you are the one who flees or fights back when you feel pushed into a corner, you, too, are not getting your needs met. Your style is also ineffective.

We all blow it once in awhile. We all get emotionally overloaded from time to time. Rather than judging your partner or yourself, it is important to keep focusing on how you can help yourselves to become more effective communicators and partners. When you are emotionally overloaded or heated, if you sense your child self or critical parent self emerge, take a time-out. It is important to calm down and clear your mind. Then you can start afresh—fully using all of your Big Picture partnering skills and communicating in a way that makes you feel effective and proud of both yourself and your partner.

HOW TO TAKE A TIME-OUT

Taking a time-out needs to be okay in any relationship, but especially if you are building a rock-solid and successful Big Picture partnership. Sometimes you need space. Sometimes you need to think. Sometimes there is something else you need to attend to before you can work on resolving a problem with your partner. Sometimes you are shutting down and can't hear clearly or respond with grace and dignity. Sometimes one of you is talking too loudly, too emotionally, and needs to put the brake on, to step back and take a big, deep breath.

In Big Picture partnering, to have effective communication in stressful times, the time-out rules are as follows:

If you feel you are verbally out of control or are shutting down and retreating, you are responsible for saying, "I need a time-out."

Both partners must automatically agree to the other's need for a time-out—no questions asked, no further statements—even if this is frustrating.

The person taking the time-out must come back to the discussion when they say they will, and when both partners are calmer.

Initially, it may be difficult for either person to follow these rules. If you know, however, that you have the option to make your communication more effective by taking or giving a time-out, it will make sense. Especially when two people agree to honor these time-out rules, they learn to trust that their partner:

- Won't chase after them and demand to talk if they are not ready or emotionally overloaded;

- Will come back and resume the conversation or resolve the issue when they feel calmer. The person taking the time-out must eventually resume the discussion and, if possible, say when they will be ready to talk again. For example, "Honey, I am shutting down and need a time-out now, but I really want to talk about this. I need to go walk around the block. Let's talk about this . . . in an hour . . . this afternoon . . . tonight after the kids are in bed . . . tomorrow evening when I'm more rested."

Taking a time-out also allows partners to drop petty disagreements that arise. Sometimes, by the time they have resumed the discussion, neither can remember what they were fighting about. Or sometimes they have thought it through and can easily resolve the issue if it is small. When issues are complex or heated, I recommend holding off until both partners are calm then they are ready to use the Intentional Dialogue technique.

Let's summarize here. Healthy resolution is acquired when partners:

- Stop the arguments and fights that have not been working.

- Follow basic respectful communication guidelines outlined earlier in "Common Communication Wisdom."

- Use time-outs as an effective means of stopping behavior that inhibits communication, such as "shutting down" or talking too heatedly.

- Become trustworthy and impeccably accountable for resuming a discussion, if you are the one who initiated the time-out.

In closing these thoughts for week 9, let me recommend a wonderful, inexpensive book that will help your partnership almost immediately: *The Two Step: The Dance Toward Intimacy,* written by Eileen McCann and delightfully illustrated by Douglas Shannon. On the book's jacket, Virginia Satir writes:

> *I find this book to be a pictorial treasure of how we act, showing the games we play while trying to hide what we want. Out of these pictures comes a clear visualization of what we are doing. With that realization, we can laugh at ourselves and be inspired to make the changes we need to make.*

In a brief thirty-minute reading, this little book illustrates the push and pull, the fight and flight, the desire and the distance we create in our relationship dramas. Get it and read it!

EXERCISES

How Do You Currently Resolve Conflicts— and What Part Do You Play?

At the beginning of the week, spend time individually reflecting on how you and your partner resolve (or fail to resolve) conflicts. Write in your journal. Ask yourself, "How do we disagree?" Are bad feelings and needs left hanging in the air, clouding the good times between you? What is your approach to dealing with conflict? What is your partner's approach? (For example, do one or both of you yell, scream, holler, or "pursue" your partner for answers? Do either of you withdraw, feel defeated or overwhelmed?)

Once you have identified your approaches to handling conflict, write about what you would like to change. What would you like each of you to do differently?

Before you discuss specific communication changes with your partner, take some time to reflect on your own willingness to change your pattern of conflict and conflict resolution. This is a hard one to face. We often want to blame the other person. Or we want to wait for the other person to change first. For example, we tell ourselves, "If only they'd stop yelling at me, then I'd come forth and give them a hug." Or, "If only they'd say something kind before telling me what they think I should do differently, it would be so much easier." What I'd like you to do here is consider what YOU would have to do differently to change the pattern of conflict resolution in your partnership.

When you are ready, make a commitment to changing the part you play in arguments with your partner. Use these four questions to clarify this commitment.

1. Am I committed to doing my part to communicate respectfully and effectively in disagreements with my partner? Am I willing to hold my tongue, if necessary? Am I willing to take time-outs if I need them? Am I willing to stay in my adult self in order to enhance our interactions?
2. What are four concrete steps I can take toward better resolving our disagreements, large or small?
3. How might I sabotage or get in the way of resolving disagreements effectively?
4. What am I willing to change, starting this week?

Your Desire to Resolve Conflicts

Now, spend time discussing these patterns of conflict and conflict resolution with your partner. Ask yourselves: How do we resolve conflict now? What patterns emerge? How would we like to do things differently? Share the changes each of you is willing to make. Take turns asking the Four Questions and listen to your partner's desire to change.

Your Need for Time-Outs

Individually, reflect on the need for time-outs in your partnership. Does one of you storm out while the other wants to pursue the disagreement? Or are you both able to stay and discuss your differences respectfully? If not, would you be willing to take a time-out as a way to improve your communication?

Discuss this during your regular talking time. Make an agreement to follow the time-out rules (found on page 200) even if you only need them once in awhile. They are useful rules to have in your back pocket, especially during times of stress.

Identifying Unresolved Issues

You'll begin this exercise this week. You will clarify your answers in the coming week's activities.

For now, do this exercise on your own. I will tell you when and how to share this with your partner in week 10.

In order to create a rock-solid foundation for your partnership, your task in the coming weeks is to:

- Discuss difficult recurring issues and create Big Picture solutions to these old problems together.
- Review how you are handling the daily details of your life—chores, finances, sexuality, schedules, kids' activities, and adult social lives— and discuss the problematic aspects of each. Then come up with creative solutions together. Daily details should become the smooth-functioning background to a more joyous and exciting life together.
- Spend some time on your own this week, writing in your journal about areas in your partnership that you feel require change, creative problem solving, or improvement. What would make your partnership rock solid? Save your list or journal notes for the coming week's exercises.

. . . .

Heartfelt Speech, Heartfelt Listening

Practicing Big Picture communication

This week you will practice resolving conflicts using the Intentional Dialogue. This is one half of Big Picture partnering Essential #10. The other half is creating new options together through creative and imaginative thought. For this, you will sometimes use the dialogue.

In weeks 10 and 11, you will learn the basic Intentional Dialogue technique and apply it to anything unresolved in your relationship and to solidifying the daily details.

In weeks 12 through 15 you will add creative methods, not only to enhance your problem-solving ability, but to actively communicate and work toward bigger dreams and goals together.

The Intentional Dialogue is a technique for communicating, especially around topics that are difficult to hear or understand. It is a tool for listening deeply to what another person is saying. It is a tool for signaling that you have heard what the other person has said and intended—through mirroring back, in a very specific way, your partner's words and eventually their feelings. It is a tool that helps you avoid making assumptions about what the other person is saying, so you can truly know what your partner thinks and feels. Using this tool will give each of you an opportunity to thoroughly explore and articulate all of your thoughts without being interrupted or cut off. We seldom have the opportunity to be listened to so well; in Big Picture partnering, the Intentional Dialogue gives you both that chance.

When it is your turn to assume the listener role, you will hear beyond your personal assumptions and realize that, "Oh, I thought you were going to say this, but I heard something different this time." You may hear new things that you didn't know your partner even thought about. You may find great wisdom, some tough feedback, some deep hurts, and even great new ideas if you learn to listen actively and well.

Once you get the hang of the Intentional Dialogue, you will find that conflicts get resolved more quickly and smoothly. In addition, because your energy is not bound up in fighting or disagreements, you will unleash more energy for play, passion, fun, and even greater creativity in your relationship.

THE INTENTIONAL DIALOGUE TECHNIQUE AND ITS USES

The Intentional Dialogue is a specific set of communications and rules about communicating compiled by Harville Hendrix and his colleagues. It was originally developed in what is called Imago Therapy. Back in the early 1970s when Parent Effectiveness Training (PET) was a new and popular communication training approach, some of the foundations of the Intentional Dialogue technique were first introduced. Over the years, various educators have used the terms *paraphrasing, mirroring,* and *active listening* to describe aspects of this healthy approach to communication. Hendrix compiled and combined the best of what was known about these tools, set a format with rules, and named the technique. It is now widely used. In my own work with partners, the Intentional Dialogue has become pivotal in helping Big Picture partners resolve conflict.

In the Big Picture approach, the Intentional Dialogue is taken one step further. Big Picture partners learn to use the Intentional Dialogue, then add to it using additional creative methods of brainstorming, building on one another's ideas, and creating new options together. What you create together might be a project, a new adventure, or an exciting plan for the next ten-year phase of your relationship. Using the Intentional Dialogue in this way, you can take time to talk about your dreams. You can reflect on one another's "wild and crazy" or new ideas without judgment. Simply listening to one another and witnessing one another's creative ideas allows you to move into new territories that you may not have explored before.

I have seen couples make monumental creative leaps in their lives, doing things they at first thought almost impossible. Olivia and Hans are one couple with a creative story to tell. Hans remarks:

Once we solidified our partnership, Olivia and I started to fantasize about having a home in the country with a few acres. She's an artist. She wanted to raise sheep for her weavings and maybe herbs to sell to fine restaurants.

Olivia chimed in:

We had looked at property earlier in our marriage, when this dream was alive and fresh. Over the years nothing seemed within our price range or close enough to family, and our dream faded. But partnering opened up creativity we had forgotten about.

Says Hans:

I was totally unconvinced that we would ever move from the city, just because I work for a big technical company and couldn't imagine what I would do living on a farm. But as we talked and listened and explored and experimented with ideas and plans, and looked at property, and talked to other people, it all started to seem more possible—all except my work!

Olivia recalls:

I remember all of our friends had to almost force you to talk to your boss about telecommuting. And he agreed almost immediately! You were so surprised!

Replies Hans:

It's true. My boss said yes on the condition I'd come in to the office two days a week—and again, that seemed like an obstacle to me. But Big Picture partnering kept us open to possibilities, and wouldn't you know, this farm came available three months later and we moved shortly after that.

Olivia says:

I love living in the country. We are close to Hans' parents, who are getting older, and he stays in the city one night a week and works from home the remaining time. It's as close to our ultimate dream as anyone can get!

Hans and Olivia have developed a solid Big Picture partnership. They started by working on their daily details. Once their "house was in order," their creative juices flowed right into planning the life they had once dreamed of—before the dream was buried. This can happen for you, too.

LEARNING THE INTENTIONAL DIALOGUE TECHNIQUE

When training couples in the use of the Intentional Dialogue, I initially spend about two hours reviewing the process and rules. Each partner takes turns being coached in their roles as "speaker" and "listener." The couple has come to the coaching session with one or two safe but meaty topics they might like to discuss. Together they decide which of these to use for practice. You two will use the same approach.

Sometimes one partner is shy about their role, or they don't always follow the rules. And, sometimes, they want to edit their partner's comments.

> The more quickly you accept and follow the rules of the Intentional Dialogue and are willing to practice this technique, the more quickly you will learn to creatively and successfully handle stressful, difficult, or long-term issues.

I have seen many couples who have applied the Intentional Dialogue change dramatically and consistently—in their communication, their closeness, and eventually in their ability to unleash creativity —within two to three weeks!

I have also worked with couples who use the technique sporadically, fail to really follow the rules, or act shy and silly (the child self) when asked to practice. These couples do not make much progress in their ability to communicate or become creative together.

When couples embrace the entire Big Picture approach and begin to use the Intentional Dialogue, they tend to use it quite often in the beginning. Eventually, the full dialogue is used only as needed. This is because couples incorporate the skills of the dialogue—listening, mirroring, validating, and empathizing—into all of their communications. You will learn how to do this as you practice this technique.

Melanie and Greg, both previously married and now engaged to each other and in their mid-thirties, had practiced partnering for about six months when they went to the flea market one Sunday and came back to report a success story. Said Melanie:

> *We've been working to communicate really well about everything in our lives as we head into marriage this fall. Everything from getting our individual and joint financial agreements in order, to picking out the new house, to sharing more sexually, to planning our family's involvement in the ceremony itself—and a million other things we've had to agree on!*

Greg said:

> *Some of these topics have been tough to get through.*

Melanie added:

> *Or they just took a long time for the two of us to talk about—to hear each other out and come to a win/win decision together. But we have to report our mutual satisfaction—even a bit of gloating—that we were able to apply all of our Big Picture skills, and especially a quick Intentional Dialogue, to decide on this fabulous dining room set we found at the flea market!*

Greg agreed.

> *I know it may seem like a little thing, but it was an unexpected and big purchase, and also a creative one for this new home of ours. Within five minutes we reviewed our finances, our values and goals about the house, and how this dining room set fit into that bigger picture. We checked out our mutual pleasure in how it looks, and even who would be responsible for getting it home! It was like a little microcosm of everything we have learned as we applied it to this delightful purchase.*

Said Melanie:

> *We feel like we're truly partners—and so quickly!*

Melanie and Greg's use of the Intentional Dialogue technique was honed to a mere five-minute exchange as they decided to purchase the flea market dining room set. This exchange took place on a solid foundation of high positive interaction and regular and respectful communication. In addition, they had practiced Big Picture partnering so they were clear about finances, dreams, and goals, both large and small. The stage was set! So when they unexpectedly found the dining room table at the flea market, it was easy to quickly run through the specifics of their conversation to arrive at their decision.

I encourage you to include this powerful and inclusive technique in your repertoire of partnering skills. It will help you in times of stress and conflict, in times of decision making, and when you are creating something new.

Now let me walk you through the Intentional Dialogue process itself. Then I will review the rules for using it in your partnership.

THE INTENTIONAL DIALOGUE PROCESS

There are three basic steps to the Intentional Dialogue:
1. mirroring,
2. validating, and
3. empathizing.

1. Mirroring

In the Intentional Dialogue, there is a speaker and a listener. They agree on the amount of time allotted for a dialogue. It is preferable if the speaker can talk until they are finished, and say everything they want to bring up, but this is not always feasible. In your beginning practice, try to set aside enough undisturbed time for each of you to speak as long as you need to.

The speaker gets to talk about anything that is important to them. Not only do they get to talk as long as they want, they even get to repeat themselves as they explore the issue. The goal of the speaker is to talk until they feel they have been fully "heard" by the listener.

The role of the listener is to do just that—to listen and then to "mirror back" what they have heard their partner say. Mirroring back involves using similar, but not necessarily the same, words—much like a paraphrase. What is most important here is that the listener attempt to listen empathically, as if in the speaker's shoes. So the listener needs to set aside their personal ego in order to understand what their partner is saying, from their partner's point of view. Then their task is to feed this message back to the speaker in words that show they have understood their partner. For example:

> Susan: "I don't like it when you go to bed without saying goodnight."

> Tom: "I hear you saying that you're unhappy with me when I forget to say goodnight to you before I go to bed."

> Susan: "That's right."

Now, mirroring is different than "editorializing." An editorial comment would be, "Oh, I know just what you mean. I've felt that way myself," or "I've seen you do that when you. . . ." When we editorialize or add our own comments and experience, we take the speaker out of their personal experience. Your task as listener is to feed back what you are hearing your partner communicate to you.

This time is for the speaker. The beauty of it is that when it is your turn, you will be listened to just as respectfully.

There are not many opportunities in life to truly think out loud and hear your deepest self communicate your thoughts, then have those thoughts reflected back so that you can get to the essence—the core— of what is important to you. Too often people will interrupt, think they know what you are saying, make assumptions about where your thought is going, or think of what they are going to say while you are still talking.

> So, step 1 is for the listener to mirror back what the speaker is saying. The listener does this until the speaker is finished sharing their thoughts.

You can help one another with just a few simple phrases. As the listener, you might say, "tell me more," if the speaker indicates that your mirroring wasn't quite correct, or, "let me see if I've got that," when the speaker has talked so long that you can hold no more thoughts and need to feed them back. Sometimes a little hand gesture, signaling for them to pause so you can mirror back what they've already said, also helps.

> **When you are the speaker, you must give clear feedback to the listener about how much you feel understood.**

For some, to be understood 70 percent is enough; others may need to be understood 93.33 percent. While this need varies, I encourage couples new at this technique to make sure they really feel like their partner is getting the essence of what they are saying. This challenges both parties to become better at listening and clarifying their communication and this effort will pay off in the ensuing work they do.

So, the speaker might say something like, "I know you are saying the right words, but something in the way you are repeating it back to me makes me feel like you don't quite have my full meaning. Let me try to say this a different way. . . ."

I have coached couples who went back and forth like this for thirty minutes until they both had the "ahhhhhhhhh"—the "inner knowing"—that the listener had finally heard the speaker's thoughts as if the listener were standing in the speaker's shoes! The difference in how you express meaning may be subtle, but when you actively listen to each other and truly hear what the other person is saying, the experience of understanding and clarity is powerful.

If the speaker hasn't fully been understood yet, they might say, "You have the first half of what I said correct, but you forgot the second point I made. Let me say it again," or, "As I hear you repeat that, I realize it isn't what I mean at all. Let me say what I really mean."

The listener's task is to pay close attention and follow the speaker's train of thought, wherever it may lead.

When the speaker finishes, when he or she feels fully understood, then the listener does two things. The first is called validating, and the second is called empathizing.

2. Validating

Validating is a simple statement made by the listener after mirroring what the speaker has said. It lets the speaker know they are making sense.

This needs to be done without repeating back any of what was previously said, and without editorializing. It is a short statement that says, "You make sense."

A few examples of validating statements would be:

> *"From everything you've told me, your experience is understandable."*
> *"You are making sense to me. I've got it."*

Adding additional comments, like the following, is not part of an Intentional Dialogue:

> *"I've got it! Gosh, and now I understand why you always get mad and throw a fit the way you do!"*

> *"I can really understand your experience, but don't you think if you knew how much I really loved you this wouldn't matter?"*

Once again, it is important to listen to the speaker's experience nonjudgmentally, removing your ego and reactions from the dialogue.

3. Empathizing

Empathizing is the final step in the Intentional Dialogue process. This is a simple statement in which the listener mirrors back the feelings that have been named by the speaker or, if no feelings have been named, the feelings they sense are revealed in the speaker's words. If the listener is off base, this may segue back into another little round of mirroring until there is again full understanding. Here are two examples of empathizing. The first example shows simple clarity.

Listener:

Everything you are saying makes sense, and I can hear just how frustrated and angry you are, how it even makes you want to give up.

Speaker:

Yes! That's exactly how I've been feeling.

In the second example, the speaker clarifies their feelings:

Listener:

Gee, honey, from everything you are saying, I get it. I can imagine that you must be feeling very sad and distant from me as a result.

Speaker:

Actually, I no longer feel sad about it. I've gotten to the point where your lack of communicating just makes me downright mad. I don't deserve to be treated this way. So I'm clear, I'm just not going to throw a tantrum anymore even though I'm mad. And I am only going to do my part in the communicating process. Otherwise we won't grow together.

Listener:

Let me see if I've got that. You're not really sad. You've become resolved. You are really angry, but you are not going to yell about it anymore. You are clear. You're not going to take my passivity or fear or stubbornness as your problem anymore. You want me to know that either I communicate or we won't have the kind of relationship we both say we want. Did I get that right?

Speaker:

You bet! That's exactly what I'm saying!

Listener:

That's exactly what you mean. Is there more?

Speaker:

No. I feel finished.

Listener again validates:

Once again, you make even more sense and I hear you.

Empathizes:

And you made it clear you are feeling mad and resolute."

Speaker:

That's for sure!

In the best scenario, the partners would then exchange roles and go through the entire process with the other person being mirrored, validated, and empathized with. If this is not possible, they agree to give the previous listener, within two days, a turn to be the speaker.

THE INTENTIONAL DIALOGUE PROCESS

I. MIRRORING

In the Intentional Dialogue, there is a speaker and a listener. Together they agree on the amount of time allotted for a dialogue. In your beginning practice, try to set aside enough undisturbed time for one of you to speak as long as you need to.

The speaker gets to talk about anything that is important to them. The goal of the speaker is to talk until they feel they have been fully "heard" by the listener until they feel finished.

The role of the listener is to listen and then to "mirror back" what they have heard their partner say. Mirroring back involves using similar, but not necessarily the same, words—much like a paraphrase. What is most important here is that the listener attempt to listen from inside the speaker's shoes. So the listener needs to set aside their personal ego—their judgments and edits—in order to understand what their partner is saying, from their partner's point of view. Then their task is to feed this message back to the speaker in words that show they have understood what their partner said.

2. VALIDATING

Validating is a simple statement made by the listener after mirroring what the speaker has said. It lets the speaker know they are making sense.

This needs to be done without repeating back any of what was previously said, and without editorializing. It is a short statement that says, "You make sense."

> *From everything you've told me, your experience is understandable. I hear you.*

> *You are making sense to me. I've got it.*

Once again, it is important to listen to the speaker's experience nonjudgmentally, removing your ego, edits, and reactions from the dialogue.

3. EMPATHIZING

Empathizing is the final step in the Intentional Dialogue. This is a simple statement in which the listener mirrors back the feelings that have been named by the speaker or, if no feelings have been named, the feelings they sense are revealed in the speaker's words. If the listener is off base, this may segue back into another little round of mirroring until there is again full understanding. The partners then exchange roles and go through the entire process with the other person being mirrored, validated, and empathized with, either within the same sitting or within two days.

ASSUMPTIONS AND UNDERSTANDING

In close relationships, people often mistakenly assume that they are listening to each other and hearing what they say. When a couple finds they have been facing unresolved issues for a period of time, they often discover through the Intentional Dialogue that they are laboring under mismatched assumptions. One partner may not have truly agreed to a particular resolution or decision. They may have been silent, or grunted, or rolled their eyes or looked at the floor. But they may never truly have said "yes" or "no." I always think that not saying "yes" should be taken as "no" more than a "maybe, we'll see, but we need to talk more" —or as a "no, for now."

The Intentional Dialogue is a magical tool for communicating. Very often couples can't arrive at a resolution on a particular issue. But, once one person feels understood, what was once problematic is no longer so. Often in our closest intimate relationships we just want to be understood; we may think we need to get our partner to agree with us, but really we just want them to hear our point of view and accept it, not diminish it or sweep it under the rug.

USING THE INTENTIONAL DIALOGUE
IN YOUR PARTNERSHIP

In the initial stages of practicing the Intentional Dialogue, use this technique at least once or twice each week for one to two months. In the beginning, set aside an hour for each dialogue.

Eventually you will mirror, validate, and empathize as a frequent part of your everyday communication. When you reach that point, in only three situations will you need to do a formal Intentional Dialogue.

The first is if one of you requests a dialogue.

It doesn't matter why. The immediate Big Picture response is, "Okay, when shall we schedule a time? I'll be there." No questions asked. No hemming and hawing. If it is important to one of you, it is important to the partnership. Remember, Essential #9: be willing to address any problem in your relationship together—*yours, mine,* or *ours.*

The second situation is if a stressful or problematic issue arises that causes you to revert to fighting.

This situation will be more easily resolved if you use the Intentional Dialogue the minute you sense a fight beginning. If you are too angry or heated, take a time-out or cool down first. Then agree to use the dialogue when you are both ready to listen.

The third circumstance is a fun one.

When you have exciting life-transition goals, big events, or creative projects you are planning, the dialogue may help you speed the positive change. Sharing goals and ideas becomes smooth and safe. You can listen to one another calmly.

EXERCISES

The Intentional Dialogue takes time and practice to master. Let's break it down into some doable steps.

Getting Acquainted

Individually, thoroughly read the Intentional Dialogue section.

Then, come together and take turns reading it aloud to one another. Discuss your understanding of the three-step process: mirroring, validating, and empathizing. Be sure to carefully review the rules for using the Intentional Dialogue and discuss what you each think it means to be an active listener.

Next, as you go about your lives, notice the conversations you overhear and participate in where the Intentional Dialogue might be helpful.

Then, in everyday interactions, start to practice and play with mirroring—but not so much that it becomes annoying. Just once in awhile start to adopt the mirroring language: "Just making sure, Hon. You want me to put the kids to bed tonight, right?" Start to use it in conversations.

Practice

Schedule two times this week to practice the Intentional Dialogue with each other. Set aside at least one uninterrupted hour for each practice session.

When you take your turn as speaker, you will share your thoughts about what the two of you need to do to create a rock-solid partnership. When you are the listener, you will practice mirroring while you listen carefully to what your partner says is needed to make your relationship rock solid.

Decide who will be the first speaker. The speaker will have thirty minutes to talk while the listener practices mirroring, validating, and empathizing. Then you will switch roles.

Due to the time limit, you may not complete a full Intentional Dialogue. That is fine; this time is mainly for practice.

If you feel you have run out of things to say, still practice for the entire thirty minutes. You can do these four things to expand on your thoughts:

1. Repeat your points using more examples and new words.
2. Go deeper—talk about how unresolved issues or daily details make you feel.
3. Make sure you talk about how you would like your relationship to be if these things were no longer problems.
4. Tell your partner what other interests you'd like the two of you pursue if the daily details flowed like clockwork.

As you practice the Intentional Dialogue, pause and start over if . . .

- You lose your train of thought as the speaker or forget where you are in the Intentional Dialogue process.
- Your ego gets in the way or you get angry as the listener. If this happens, pause and note what you are feeling. Don't act inappropriately or say anything. Breathe, and remember, you will have a turn to speak. When you are ready, return to active listening.
- You find yourself editing the speaker by adding your own comments, thoughts, or interpretations—rather than being mirroring, validating, and empathizing.

After each practice session, do not debrief. Allow yourselves to absorb what you have shared.

Two days later, do another Intentional Dialogue during which you discuss the same issues you raised in the last session. The partner who went second last time will go first this time.

Then, do something playful or out-of-the-ordinary together.

. . . .

Goals of the Heart

Setting a course for the destination you most desire

In week 11, you are going to put your heads together and make a list of goals that, once achieved, will solidify your Big Picture partnership.

> Resolving conflicts and building a more rock-solid and creative partnership—applying your skills to smooth out the daily details of your life together—should be the hallmark of your Big Picture goals in the coming weeks. You will apply all 10 Essentials, along with some additional creative methods, to the list of goals you establish together.

As you resolve conflicts and build more harmony
in handling the daily details, you will then add
new goals that are about your bigger dreams.

You have a lot to accomplish this week, so pace yourselves.

WHAT ARE THE UNRESOLVED ISSUES INHIBITING YOUR ROCK-SOLID PARTNERING FOUNDATION?

You may already be a good goal-setter. Or maybe you are one of those people who doesn't like to set goals, or know how to. Common wisdom shows that people who set goals achieve more in life. I also find that if you have two people trying to accomplish something together, they need to synchronize their efforts, to set their sights on the same target. Those who clarify what they want and decide how they will work to achieve their dreams will do just that.

If you are not in the habit of setting goals, try these exercises and experiment so you can see the positive changes you create together. If you have experience with goal setting, this is the beginning of a process to help you synchronize your goals and accomplish them together as partners. This is a process that can ultimately bring more connectivity and creativity into your life.

YOUR GOALS: ARE THEY NEEDS, DESIRES, OR DREAMS?

As you grow, you each have the opportunity to provide for yourself and others at two levels. The first is a basic survival level. These are needs for food, clothing, and shelter. You may also need a bit of money, and bodies, enjoy sex. The second level involves things you want. You may not need that red dress or new Porsche, but you may want it! Unlike survival needs, which, if unmet, can result in illness or even death, wants can be modified. You may want a feast, but a steak sandwich may do. You may want a two-week vacation, but a day by the lake may better fit your schedule and budget—and give you the downtime you want.

Then there are the wants that some people think of as "abundance" or "havingness." Allowing yourself this kind of wealth may or may not involve money. Such abundance may relate to your wealth of knowledge, wisdom, friends, or laughter, or your connection to God, a Higher Being, nature, or beauty. This is where your dreams and desires come into play.

EXERCISES

The exercises for week 11 offer many opportunities for thinking, writing, and communicating about your goals. Set aside at least one hour a day to work on these exercises.

For the first three days, do the exercises individually. Don't talk about your goals with your partner until at least day 4.

Your One-Year Goals

Your Big Picture partnering universe includes *my goals, your goals,* and *our goals.* If you have a family, our goals include what you mutually want for your family. Start to write about your individual goals, couple goals, and, if applicable, family goals, for one year from today. As you do so, remember that individual, couple, and family goals need to work together in the universe. You might use separate sheets of paper, or separate columns on one sheet.

Your individual goals are what you'd like to accomplish personally this year: these goals would be in your work, for your health and exercise, etc. Then, think about how you want your relationship to be one year from now. (Imagine that all the issues are largely or entirely resolved and that the daily details of your relationship are being handled smoothly and effortlessly. Your goals would describe the positive outcomes you desire and what you would be doing together to accomplish them.) Finally, what do you desire for your entire family? (This might include vacations and activities together, spending time learning something new together, etc.)

To help you write these one-year goals, think about the goals you'd like to set in every area of your life:

- Your partnership
- Parenting
- Extended family
- Friendships
- Social life and activities
- Work life
- Spiritual life
- Creative pursuits
- Physical health, exercise
- Sex life
- Finances and investments—short-term and long-term
- Everyday household upkeep and maintenance
- Household projects, renovation, or remodeling
- Intellectual or learning activities
- Fun and leisure
- Travel
- Other

Give yourself some time, in a particularly nice setting, to consider these aspects of your life. Go somewhere overlooking a lake or the ocean, curl up in your favorite chair, or take yourself out to your favorite coffee shop for a few hours. Take a written list of the above categories and any others that fit your circumstances.

The first time through, allow your mind to wander for a while. Now ask yourself, "How do I want our life to be a year from now?" What do you want:

- For yourself—as an individual
- Within your partnership—as a couple
- Within your family (if applicable)

Then start to write about what you need or want, fleshing out each of the categories on your list. Include:

- Things you appreciate and want to continue
- Things you wish to resolve or change between you
- Things you want to add or create

Be especially mindful that you are trying to establish a solid Big Picture universe. Ask yourself the following questions: If we are to establish a rock-solid and creative Big Picture universe within a year, what do I need to do? What do we need to do within the coming months? What do we need to do for our family?

Some people write a few paragraphs describing their overall goals, or what they project their lives will feel and look like in one year. Others make lists.

Be sure to include all the little and big things that you desire to manifest in the coming year. For example:

> *I want a weekend vacation, alone with my husband, without the kids, next summer. We need some time on our own.*

> *I want to start looking for a new job in six months, once I have learned what I set out to learn at this company. I need to talk to my partner about this.*

> *I want us to continue practicing being more emotionally mature. I want us to continue becoming better communicators. I want us to feel more connected to each other by this time next year.*

> *I want to eat more healthy foods and get more exercise and rest. I am a happier person and partner when I do this.*

I want us to find a way to resolve disagreements about the children's bedtime and discipline. I'd rather spend our evenings relaxing and talking together.

I want to continue sticking to my budget and even have money saved by the end of the year. I would feel proud of myself if I accomplished that. It would contribute to our partnership.

Next weekend, I want to buy those red boots I saw yesterday at the mall.

I want to resolve our lack of sexual intimacy. We seem to be going through the motions these days.

This summer I want more time to golf or fish.

I want to feel closer to God. I'd like to talk more about our spiritual life.

I want to spend more time with my parents now that they are getting older and less active. I don't know how long they have to live and I don't want any regrets. I'm not sure how to balance this with my family, but I'd like my partner to support me in this.

Identify six or seven of your top goals, across the three categories. Star or circle them. Then, let your mind wander over all the possible things you could do to accomplish each goal. Don't censor or limit your ideas. Some ideas may be practical, some may be wild and crazy. At this point it doesn't matter.

Again, for three days, do not share your thoughts. Simply write down your ideas, put them by your bedside, and read them over before going to sleep each night. As ideas come to you throughout the day, write them down.

Three Individual Goals

Next, choose three short-term goals from your list. These should be high priorities for you, but ones toward which you could make significant progress within five weeks. Using your journal, write out these three goals clearly. For example:

- My goal is to start getting back in shape by committing to go to the gym for one hour three times each week for the next five weeks. My ultimate vision is to continue doing this throughout the year so that within twelve months I lose ten pounds and can get back into last year's jeans!

- During the coming year, my vision is to develop a better balance between personal, family, and work time. I am committed to using the next five weeks to experiment with a few options toward accomplishing that goal. One is to go in to the office one hour earlier three days a week, close my door for that hour, and use that quiet time to get through my paperwork. This will enable me to leave work earlier and spend more time on the things that I enjoy, including being with my partner and my family. I also plan on delegating more of the detail work to my assistant and will set up one meeting with her each week to accomplish this. In order to ensure that I keep more reasonable hours, I will let my staff know I am leaving by five o'clock at least four nights a week, and I will ask my wife to join me downtown for an early dinner date one night each week.

Once you have clearly written down your goals, ask yourself about each goal, "What are the obstacles to accomplishing this goal? How might I sabotage myself or get in my own way of accomplishing this goal?" Write about all this. If you like, talk it over with a friend who listens well.

Then, review your list of all the possible ways you could achieve your goals, and write down all the small action steps you could take in each case. Make a commitment to work toward the goals in a realistic way. Highlight three or four small steps you are willing to take toward your goal in the next two weeks. Choose two that you will start today and/or later this week. Continue to work toward this goal for the next five weeks.

Share Your Goals with Your Partner

Come together and take turns reading your lists slowly out loud to one another. Listen carefully.

Once you have shared all your goals, discuss your responses. Are your goals aligned? Talk about any surprises—not in a judgmental way, but by sharing your reactions. Talk about these lists in terms of your values and priorities, what you desire in partnering, and what you each feel needs to be improved or added to make your partnership rock solid.

Make a Combined Master List of One-Year Goals

Now you'll create a master list of partnership goals (and, if appropriate, family goals) for the year to come.

Here is an opportunity to clarify your mutual goals in a common language. Use the Intentional Dialogue to mirror one another, making sure that the intentions, needs, and desires that each of you share are noted in your master list.

One of you may have something on your list that the other person does not. Here is an opportunity to discuss if this goal is truly acceptable to both parties. For example, a husband may wish to take a cross-country family vacation, and his wife may be more than willing to add this to their partnership goals. On the other hand, her desire to spend money on an addition to the house within the next year may be seen as financially out of the question. In this event, they have two options. One is to postpone the addition until a later time—and perhaps put it on a three-year goal list. Another is to decide on a one-year goal that is a baby step toward the bigger goal.

Now that you have made a joint list of goals, set your lists of individual goals alongside this master list.

Our master list of goals

YOUR GOALS	PARTNERING GOALS		MY GOALS
	Couple Goals	Family Goals	
_____	_____	_____	_____
_____	_____	_____	_____
_____	_____	_____	_____
_____	_____	_____	_____
_____	_____	_____	_____
_____	_____	_____	_____
_____	_____	_____	_____

Talk about your willingness to support one another's individual goals during the coming year. Share your concerns and commitment to these individual goals. Talk about what will be required of each of you to support each other's goals. For example, if one of you wants to exercise more regularly, the other may volunteer to watch the kids one or two evenings a week, or you may need to alter your car pooling or mealtime. How can you support one another's individual needs? Some goals may be rewritten or altered in order to assure that individual goals are supported by the other partner.

Action Steps

Over the next five weeks, you will continue to work on your goals as you master Big Picture concepts and skills together.

This week you will identify specific action steps that you will take—both individually and as a couple—toward accomplishing your goals in these weeks.

Spend some time talking about the progress you'd each like to make toward the goals you have set for the coming five weeks. Use the Intentional Dialogue, either formally or informally.

With the five-week period in mind, together choose the top three priorities from each of three lists: your two individual lists and your joint master list. These are the goals you are willing to work on—*your goals, my goals,* and *our goals*—during weeks 12 through 16. If you have a family, you will also choose one family goal from your master list.

Since you'll want to make progress and feel successful, choose two less difficult goals and only one more complex or more challenging goal from your master list.

For example, altering your meal planning/grocery shopping regimen may be a less complex goal than improving your sex life—although both may be on your individual and/or master goal lists. Finding a mutually satisfying way of handling money—from paying bills to establishing savings and investment plans—is often a loaded and difficult issue, but an important one to tackle in order to have a good partnering foundation and create smooth-functioning daily details. In fact, I suggest that you select "smoother handling of finances" as your complex goal.

Especially for complex goals, try to establish a series of specific actions you can take in the next five weeks. For example,

> *One year from now we would like to be in full agreement and well informed about all aspects of our money management. As a solid step toward this, we agree that in the next five weeks we will review our current financial status, then have weekly meetings to continue doing so. We will also get the names of three financial planners and make appointments with at least two of them.*

During the past eleven weeks you have upped the positives in your relationship. If the positives continue to outweigh the negatives, and if your communication skills continue to improve, you'll likely find that difficult goals become easier to achieve. If you get creative together, and throw in a little humor and lots of laughter, you'll even have fun along the way.

Once you have mutually chosen your three partnering goals, brainstorm about each goal, one at a time, for ten minutes. For each goal, make a list—without judgment or edits—that includes all the possible ways you could work toward it individually and together. Write down all the specific things you can do as partners to make this goal a reality. Then, choose the three or four most practical steps. Circle those you could accomplish within the next week, then map out the steps you could take in weeks 12 through 16, so you have a clear picture of your progress.

Next, divide up the tasks: who will do what and by what date? Agree to be accountable. Agree on a weekly day and time at which you will report back to each other on your progress toward this goal. These get-togethers will now become your regular partnering meetings.

Also agree that each week you will have one additional partnering meeting during which you will discuss progress toward this goal or take a specific action step together.

After you have a plan for this first partnership goal, follow the same steps for your two remaining goals. Then do the same for your individual goals, either together or separately.

A word about family goals (if you have them). If your children are old enough, hold a family meeting to discuss all the possible ways you might work toward accomplishing a goal, such as planning a family activity or vacation, making bedtimes easier, or planning meals and cleanup better. Assign or get volunteers for tasks and agree to report back to each other at another family meeting in a week or two.

At each partnering and family meeting, use the following formula for brief follow-up (unless more conversation is required):

· Each of you gives a brief report on the action steps taken to accomplish the identified goal.
· Then, each of you talks through the four questions to: 1) define your goal this week, 2) ask for help or support, 3) identify ways you might self-sabotage, and 4) describe the action steps you plan to take this week (for each goal).

After your partnering and family meetings, spend a few moments talking about what you appreciate about each other and do something fun or memorable together: popcorn and a video, a bike ride, a back-yard water balloon fight, or a build-your-own pizza dinner.

. . . .

Two People, One Journey

Practice coming together
vs. taking sides

As you work on your individual goals, partnership goals, and family goals during weeks 12 through 15, you will become aware of little ways that you can enhance your creativity. For example, during week 12, you will be encouraged to find all the ways in which you actually come together, rather than focus on where you are different, or where you take opposing sides.

Together, you will practice this subtle shift in communicating—during your regular talking times as well as in your active listening and mirroring. Then you will add this to your exercises for the week as you work toward your individual, partnership, and family goals.

COMING TOGETHER ENHANCES YOUR CREATIVITY

Do you ever feel like you and your partner are in enemy camps? I once assigned a particularly feisty couple the task of carrying squirt guns—to remind them to "lay down their arms." They quickly learned to see the humor in how they approached one another as enemies rather than as allies. They had spent enormous amounts of time arguing over who was right and who was to blame. And it not only sucked up all their time and creative energy, it had polarized them so they could only see their differences. They guarded their individual turf very well, but they were unable to come together to build, create, or imagine anything new.

Relationships are not meant to be courtroom battles, war zones, or debate tournaments. Home should be a safe harbor where you can let your hair down, play, and be a little goofy. This rejuvenates you for going back out into the world of work and high expectations—where sometimes battles do have to be fought. When we are competitive in the rest of our lives, learning to soften when we walk in the front door takes practice.

One way to increase your creativity is to find all the ways you are similar. Of course you have differences. That is a given when two unique individuals spend time together. But rather than oppose each other, which stops the flow of creative ideas and energy—as well as the flow of trust and love, if fights are a constant—why not actively seek common ground? When you discover similarities in your thinking, desires, dreams, or goals, you will:

- Both feel more accepted, listened to, and loved.
- Establish an arena—rather than a boxing ring—in which to create what you both want in life.

Focusing on all the ways you come together, rather than all the ways you are different, will do three important things that are beneficial for your partnership. It will

- Make you feel more understood.
- Make you feel more connected.
- Remove obstacles to your mutual flow of creativity.

Think of yourselves like rivers flowing toward the equator, pulled by gravitational forces. Your individual waters flow in the same direction and seek a coming together—to form a larger, more forcefully flowing river or body of water. Your ideas, thoughts, dreams, conversations, and desires are like those waters seeking to merge; seeking to form a greater creative energy than either of you can manifest on your own.

Luis and Rosa had difficulty coming together in this way. Rosa explained it this way:

> *We've been together for almost sixteen years. In the past, whenever I came up with an idea, Luis would either tell me about three or four better ideas he'd heard of, or describe all the problems we'd run into if we pursued my idea. As a result, we never went on any trips or took any classes together. It was hard to agree on how to socialize or do anything new. I always felt like he wanted to put a boulder in our path, like he didn't love me or want to support my ideas. I sort of felt like he thought my ideas were stupid.*

Luis agreed and went on to explain the changes they have made.

> *Rosa is right. But I also thought she didn't support my ideas either. I would try to throw in my two cents when she came up with an idea, thinking it would help, but it never did. She always felt like I was*

shooting her ideas down, or trying to promote my ideas. Then I learned to just listen to Rosa. At first I had to mirror what she had said to make sure I understood. And then I practiced saying things to her that were similar to her ideas—and stopped saying things that were not similar. Gradually I realized that my whole family talks the way I used to! You say a thought or idea, and they take it in a million different directions, but never in the direction you had wanted your idea to go. They don't even realize they are doing it—but nobody's ideas ever come together as a result. Everyone in my family ends up doing things on their own.

As they learned to come together in their conversations, Luis and Rosa found that creating new things in their relationship became more frequent and easier. Rosa explained:

When we practiced focusing on our similarities, daily life became much more connected and loving. And we discovered we have things in common! For instance, Luis and I decided to take up Latin dancing and we plan regular trips every year.

Luis added:

When we were able to talk this way, my love of music and her love of movement became an obvious match—one we hadn't figured out before when I was busy coming up with my own ideas. Not to say I wasn't reluctant to go to a salsa class, but I was willing to try! Before, we couldn't even get beyond my discussion of all the different styles of music or bad dance teachers or expense of lessons. I really love to go dancing with her now.

Added Rosa:

And although we don't always get the urge to travel to the same place or at the same time, when we research an area and the possibilities, we always find something about our travel goals that satisfies both of our appetites.

As you practice coming together, the first step is to actively listen to your partner. Then, become aware of the language you use in response to your partner's ideas or thoughts. For a while, practice saying only those things that directly support or are similar to your partner's. Practice putting aside ideas that are dissimilar, and only share thoughts or ideas that flow with your partner's thoughts. You can always bring up a different idea at another time if it is important to you. Then your partner can find ways to come together with your ideas.

EXERCISES

Notice When You Polarize vs. When You Come Together

When you communicate with your partner, make a note of each time you find yourself pointing out differences, being negative about an idea, or taking an oppositional point of view. Write your observations in your journal or workbook. Ask yourself: What purpose do these polarizing comments serve for me? How can I break this habit? What do I need to do to better connect with my partner when we talk?

Practice Coming Together

As you raise your individual awareness of any polarizing or negativity, consciously practice focusing your conversations on the ways in which you are similar or in agreement. Notice these especially during your regular talking times or in dialogue about your mutual goals.

Then, during one of your regular talking times, take turns describing what you have each noticed about the quality of your communication and how each of you is working to improve it. Be sure to show your appreciation for any progress you see the two of you making.

Moving toward Your Mutual Goals

At your weekly partnering (and family) meetings, you will discuss your progress and decide on the next action steps you will take individually, as partners, or as a family as you work toward your goals. At the meetings, use the following agenda:

Each of you gives a brief report on the action steps taken so far to accomplish goal #1, then #2, and then #3:

- For each goal and action steps reported on, briefly evaluate together the progress you've made.
- Brainstorm on your options, if necessary, then choose your next action steps and state what each of you plans to do.
- Take turns using the four questions to: 1) define your goal this week, 2) ask for help or support, 3) identify ways you might self-sabotage, and 4) describe the action steps you plan to take this week (for each goal).
- Do not discuss these. Simply ask the questions and listen to one another's desired actions. Do this for each of your individual, partnership, and family goals every week from week 12 through week 15. Be realistic, but push yourselves just a bit to keep momentum going.

Moving toward Your Individual Goals

Review the three individual goals you chose in week 11, as well as the action steps you decided to begin with. Check in with yourself on your progress toward these goals. Acknowledge your progress. Then choose the action steps you will take this week toward your goals. You will report on these at the next partnering or family meeting.

As you continuously work on your goals, use the following format to evaluate your progress:

- Restate your individual goal #1 (or #2, or #3).
- Reflect on your progress so far.
- Define the steps you plan to take in the weeks to come toward accomplishing the goal.
- Identify your potential for self-sabotage as you progress toward the goal.

Each time you complete one of your goals, return to your main list of individual goals and choose the next goal you would like to work on. Then decide on your action steps toward this new goal.

Progress toward Your Partnership Goals

Continue to work together on the action steps that will help you to accomplish the three partnership goals identified in week 11, resolve difficult issues between you, and master daily details together. Remember that you are working to build a solid partnering foundation during these sixteen weeks.

Once you have completed one of your partnership goals, choose another from the list you created in week 11 and begin to work on this goal together, so that you always have three goals—two less difficult and one more complex—to focus on at all times.

When you meet to talk about your partnership goals, use the following process:

- Restate mutual partnership goal #1 (or #2 or #3).
- Reflect on your overall progress so far, first separately, then together.
- Discuss how your "coming together" has enhanced progress toward your goals this week.
- Define the steps you plan to take this week, separately and together, toward accomplishing each goal.
- Explain your own potential for sabotaging progress toward each goal. (Your partner does the same.)
- Discuss and decide on something special you will do as partners at least once this week.

Progress toward Your Family Goal

Engage in the same process for your family goal this week. Involve children in these discussions whenever appropriate.

In week 11 you chose one family goal. When you accomplish this goal, choose another family goal from the one-year goal list you created. Follow that process, including everyone in each step.

- Restate your family goal.
- Reflect on your progress so far as a family.
- Discuss how your "coming together" has enhanced progress toward your goals this week.
- Define the next action steps you will take as a family toward accomplishing your goal.
- Discuss the ways in which your family might sabotage this goal this week. (Each family member might also mention their own self-sabotage.)
- Discuss and decide on something special you plan to do as a family after your family meeting.

1 + 1 = Countless Joys and Successes

*Building on one another's
thoughts and ideas*

This week, you will practice using phrases that build on one another's ideas, goals, and dreams. You will incorporate these phrases into your regular talking times and your partnering and family meetings. See how building on one another's thoughts promotes mutual creativity.

LET ME BUILD ON THAT IDEA

This week, you will practice inserting a few additional phrases into your conversations that will further increase your ability to come together creatively.

When your partner shares an idea or a thought, once you are sure you have understood (using the mirroring technique if necessary), respond by saying:

> *Let me build on that idea. . . . Or,*
> *Would it be all right if I built on that idea?*

> *Let me add to that thought. . . . Or,*
> *Would it be all right if I added to that thought?*

As you practice this strategy, you will experience the building-block effect of reciprocal ideas being exchanged. You will create a network of interlocking ideas, rather than ideas that are conflicting, disjointed, or disconnected. You might even try to draw or map your newly interconnected ideas as you converse, in order to gain a visual picture of how your ideas relate to and enhance one another's.

This exercise is related to the notion of finding all the ways you come together, rather than focusing on ways you are dissimilar. It will help you to generate a creative flow of ideas that both of you can enthusiastically endorse.

The following are additional phrases that you can use to build on each other's ideas or thoughts. (Of course, feel free to come up with your own as well.)

> *I can see that if (refer to what your partner has just shared), then. . . .*

> *I can imagine that if we (refer to what your partner has just said), then. . . .*

I am wondering if we also. . . .

I'd like to explore that option some more and add. . . .

What if we did what you suggest and then also experimented with. . . .

Incorporate these phrases into your conversations this week. At first you may want to mimic and play, just to practice, until you each find the phrases that feel right to you. The aim is to continue to come together, build on each other's ideas, and intensify the creative flow of ideas and connection between you.

EXERCISES

Using Each Other's Ideas as Building Blocks

Practice using the phrases on pages 252–253 in all of your communications this week, especially during your partnering and family meetings. Do this playfully at first, if the suggested phrases feel awkward. Gradually, this process will become more natural as you find your own favorite phrases.

Notice if there is a difference in your conversations as you practice building creatively on each other's ideas. Also notice how the use of these phrases affect the action steps you take toward your goals. (Later in the week, share with each other what you have noticed about the use of these phrases. Also share your appreciation for one another.)

Progress toward Your Individual Goals

Review the three individual goals you chose in week 11, as well as the action steps you decided upon. Check in with yourself on your progress toward these goals. Acknowledge your progress. Then choose the action steps you will take toward your goals this week. Remember to discuss these at your partnering meeting this week.

As you continue to work toward your goals, use the following process:

- Note your individual goal #1 (or #2, or #3).
- Review your progress so far, especially during the previous week.
- Create and commit to action steps toward accomplishing your goal in the coming week.
- Note the specific ways in which you might be tempted to sabotage the process, and make a commitment to avoid such sabotage.

Each time you complete one of your goals, return to your main list of individual goals and choose the next goal you would like to work on. Set a date for when you will decide on your next action steps.

Progress toward Your Partnership Goals

Continue to work together on the action steps that will help you to accomplish the three partnership goals identified in week 11, resolve difficult issues between you, and master daily details together. Remember that you are working to build a solid partnering foundation.

Once you have completed one of your partnership goals, choose another from the list you created in week 11 and begin to work on this goal together, so that you always have three goals—two less difficult and one more complex—to focus on at all times.

As before, when you meet to talk about your partnership goals, use the following process:

- Restate your partnership goal #1 (or #2, or #3) together.
- Reflect on your progress so far.
- Define the action steps you plan to take this week, separately and together, toward accomplishing each goal.
- Each of you explain your potential for self-sabotage.
- Discuss and decide on something special you will to do this week as partners.

Progress toward Your Family Goal

Engage in the same process for your family goal this week. Involve the children whenever appropriate.

In week 11 you chose one family goal. Whenever you accomplish this goal, choose another family goal from your one-year goal list that you created. At meetings, review the following items:

- The family goal.
- Your progress so far as a family.
- The action steps you plan to take this week, individually and together, toward accomplishing your family goal.
- The potential for self-sabotage as a family. (Each family member might also explain their own potential for self-sabotage.)
- Something special you will do as a family after the meeting.

. . . .

As Your Lives Unfold

Creating change and
inventing new options together

This week you'll practice creating new options together to resolve problems, reach goals, and realize dreams.

Two heads are sometimes better than one. You each know how you'd like to handle many situations if you are on your own. This week you'll practice inventing new options together that are *mutually* desired, *mutually* chosen, and *mutually* beneficial.

When you invent new options, it gives you:

- more choice and flexibility.
- great selection and alternatives.
- more mutually agreed-upon possibilities to go into your *our world* circle.

MUTUAL OPTIONS

By now, you are familiar with the concepts of *your world, my world,* and *our world,* and you know that nothing goes into *our world* until it is fully agreed on. In practice, however, many couples hit a stumbling block when they bring their individual suggestions to the table for discussion. In an attempt to arrive at a decision, they may perceive their solution as obvious, or the only option. Or they sometimes naively imagine that their partner will be enthusiastic about their suggestion, only to be crestfallen when the other person says, "I'm sorry honey, but I don't like that idea," or "I'd rather not. That doesn't interest me."

Tim and Sophie became stuck during their discussions. They were in full agreement about their one-year goals; but, they had different ideas about how to achieve them. Tim reflected:

> *Way back in the beginning of setting our one-year goals, we both wanted to get in better shape within about six months. I had gained about thirty extra pounds and wanted to take that off. Sophie hadn't been exercising, except for chasing after our two-year-old, and we wanted to find some things to do together, because our time is limited. I was doing a lot of reading about diets and brought up an easy, but healthy diet, which I was excited about. Sophie quickly agreed to join in, and we have been doing the diet for three months now. I've lost a lot of weight and feel much better. It's easy with both of us eating the same way.*

Sophie added:

> *I was glad to do the diet. Not that I needed to lose a lot of weight, but I wanted to regulate my eating for a while and it seemed a good idea to do this together. But then, when it came to the exercise part—Tim is a fanatic! He loves to run and lift weights. I used to run, too, and he*

kept saying, "Just come running with me. It will be fun. We can do it together!"

Tim agreed:

Yeah, I really tried to twist Sophie's arm and forgot to partner. I thought she should enjoy doing it, because she used to like to run and I enjoy it. Finally, I paid attention enough to hear her trying to tell me how tired she was after taking care of the baby and how she no longer enjoyed running.

Sophie explained:

Tim finally did hear me, but then we needed some help to figure out where to go from there so we could agree on the kind of exercise approach we both wanted.

Tim and Sophie were successful in partnering on a diet because they both agreed on a method. Their different thoughts about an exercise regimen, however, led to many arguments between them. For a time, Tim was sure his idea should be adopted, and Sophie simply voiced all the reasons why this wouldn't work for her. She wanted Tim to understand her point of view. Three things were missing from Tim and Sophie's conversations that kept them from moving closer to agreement and, thus, closer to achieving their Big Picture partnering goal of getting in better shape.

- First, in trying to jump to a solution too quickly, Tim and Sophie were not engaging in dialogue and not actively listening to each other's needs.

- Second, Tim thought Sophie should simply accept an exercise form that worked for him, forgetting that Big Picture partnering requires a win/win decision.

- Third, although Sophie wanted Tim to fully understand her objections to his idea, she didn't offer any new ideas that would have promoted a dialogue toward agreement.

This partnership was stuck. They were not finding ways to come together. Each of them had to let go of their old notions of how things should be to invent new options. They often got stuck by limiting their solutions to only one or two that were obvious at the time. Remember, a duel to the death is an option. So is a shouting match. What is important about these options is that they be mutually desired, mutually chosen, and mutually beneficial.

You may find that this happens in your relationship. Then what? You might let the topic drop. It might go unresolved. Then, one of you may bring it up again, and the same old unworkable solutions are rehashed, ending with the same old stalemate. Like Tim and Sophie, and many other couples, you may forget to think creatively when you're up against a stalemate situation. Here's a new strategy that worked for them. It can work for you.

Sophie and Tim learned to mutually create new options together. When they came to the partnering table, they learned to draw *my world, your world,* and *our world* circles on a piece of paper.

After identifying their individual solutions (options A and B), they used mirroring, active listening, and brainstorming to come up with at least three new possibilities (options C, D, and E) they could both enjoy. From these many options, Sophie and Tim chose the one that pleased them most.

In this week's exercise, you will apply this same process to identify options for reaching your goals. Let me show you how this works on page 262.

You can see from the diagram that Tim's potential solution, running together, is Option A. When it was pointed out that Sophie initially failed to offer any solutions, she finally suggested:

> *I'm not interested in running or training for a race like you are, but I do like to walk, and if you would consider compromising, I'd do some brisk walking with you three times a week after dinner.*

Brisk walking became Option B; however, Tim wasn't buying it. At this point, Tim and Sophie were encouraged to keep these individual options on the table, and to come up with at least three totally different ideas. They slowly began to play with ideas together, priming the pump of their mutual creativity. It had rusted a bit after years of stalemate arguments, but as they brainstormed, their creativity began to resurface. They talked about their responses to some of the more serious ideas each had come up with. Tim said:

> *I'm wondering if we don't both need to do something totally new. I hear that Sophie wants an exercise that's challenging but not harsh and which fits into our odd schedules. And I really like a challenge.*

As they talked together, they invented new Options C, D, and E: joining a regular evening Pilates class, purchasing exercise equipment for a home gym, and taking private yoga classes. Sophie remarked:

> *Mapping out our options on paper was fun. I think we were both surprised at how difficult it was to come up with C, D, and E options, but once we narrowed down our various ideas to the three we could both enjoy, we started to get excited.*

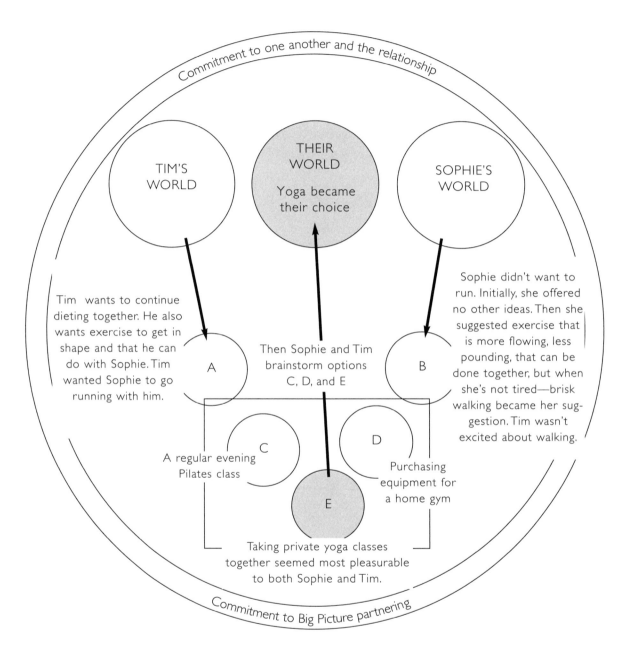

Commitment to one another and the relationship

TIM'S WORLD

THEIR WORLD

Yoga became their choice

SOPHIE'S WORLD

Tim wants to continue dieting together. He also wants exercise to get in shape and that he can do with Sophie. Tim wanted Sophie to go running with him.

A

Then Sophie and Tim brainstorm options C, D, and E

B

Sophie didn't want to run. Initially, she offered no other ideas. Then she suggested exercise that is more flowing, less pounding, that can be done together, but when she's not tired—brisk walking became her suggestion. Tim wasn't excited about walking.

C

A regular evening Pilates class

D

Purchasing equipment for a home gym

E

Taking private yoga classes together seemed most pleasurable to both Sophie and Tim.

Commitment to Big Picture partnering

Tim and Sophie's Universe
When encouraged to come up with additional creative options, Tim and Sophie generated at least three that were mutually satisfying. They agreed to experiment with yoga.

Said Tim:

> *We talked about each idea, and the private yoga instruction really excited both of us. Now we love yoga, and we can schedule the lessons any time of the day or evening.*

Sophie added:

> *Both of us love the new challenge. We can be doing the very same yoga movement, but I can go at my own pace and so can Tim. It's perfect for us.*

When, like Tim and Sophie, you can't seem to move beyond a stalemate with your partner and are unable to choose mutually agreed-upon action steps toward your goals, use the following exercises to generate new options.

EXERCISES

Practice Generating New Options

This week, as you work on your partnership goals, practice creating new options with your partner. You might want to choose a goal that has previously led to a stalemate, but don't choose something that normally results in a fight.

Be patient with each other, and try not to revert to old behaviors or polarizing. Strive to create and agree on mutually-satisfying options. Then try out the most agreeable idea together.

Here's a more detailed look at how this process might work:

Use your workbook or journal to draw your Big Picture circles. Choose your individual circles and, in your circle, write one idea on how to reach the desired goal. Your partner does the same. These are options A and B.

Stop and discuss what each of you usually does at this point that may contribute to a stalemate, or prevent the conversation from moving toward agreement.

Talk about what you each have to let go of in order to come together to find mutually satisfying options.

Then, together, brainstorm a list of eight to fifteen other possibilities. Some may be practical; some may be wild and crazy ideas. Write these on a separate sheet of paper. Discuss each new idea and identify those that best satisfy both your needs.

Then, draw three, four, or five circles floating outside the *our world* circle for options C, D, and E.

Put the top ideas into the circles labeled options C, D. and E.

Continue talking and listening to each other in order to agree on the option you would most like to try out together. This option goes into the *our world* circle.

Experiment with this option in the coming weeks, for an agreed-upon length of time, to determine if it truly helps you meet your goals. (Remember, you can always choose another option to try out later if the first one proves unsatisfying.)

Progress toward Your Individual Goals

In the coming weeks, as you continue to work toward your goals, review the following regularly:

- Your individual goal #1 (or #2, or #3).
- Your progress so far.
- The action steps you plan to take this week toward accomplishing your goal.
- Your potential for self-sabotage.

Each time you complete one of your goals, return to your main list of individual goals and choose the next goal you would like to work on. Set a date for when you will decide on your action steps. Continue refining your personal style in working toward your goals. Set your own pace. Be sure to reevaluate and refine your process, as many goals are steps along the way to our larger visions.

Progress toward Your Partnership Goals

Continue to work together on the action steps that will help you to accomplish the three partnership goals identified in week 11, resolve difficult issues between you, and master daily details together. Remember that you are working to build a solid partnering foundation.

Once you have completed one of your partnership goals, choose another from the list you created in week 11 and begin to work on this goal together, so that you always have three goals—two less difficult and one more complex—to focus on at all times.

As you continue to work toward your goals together, review the following together at meetings:

- Your partnership goal #1 (or #2, or #3).
- Your progress so far.
- The action steps you plan to take this week toward accomplishing your goals.
- Your potential for self-sabotage, individually and together.
- Something special you plan to do this week as partners.

Progress toward Your Family Goal

Engage in the same process for your family goal this week. Involve the children whenever appropriate. After you accomplish your current goal, choose another family goal from your one-year goal list that you created in week 11. At each family meeting, review the following:

- The family goal.
- Your progress so far as a family.
- The action steps you plan to take this week, individually and together, toward accomplishing your family goal.
- The potential for self-sabotage as a family, and as individuals.
- Something special you will do as a family after the meeting.

. . . .

Great Couples Are Inventors and Rule Breakers

Joyously exploring and experimenting together

Throughout these past fourteen weeks, you have been trying out many new things together. This week you will stretch even further.

You'll look at all the nooks and crannies of your life to become aware of any ways in which you may be in a rut—individually or together. For example, you may find you always drive the same roads to work or you may eat at the same old restaurant each week? You may take your family to the same resort, or have sex in the same position, or wear the same suit, or tie, to social events.

While some routines bring satisfaction, anything that is a habit may keep you from challenging your creativity. This week, your task is to notice your unconscious ruts so that you can make new choices about how you do even the smallest things in life. This week your challenge is to experiment and explore. Have fun!

THE "EXPERIMENT AND EXPLORE" FRAME OF MIND

Frequent experimenting and exploring in little ways can be fun. It also makes you resilient, ready for changes that come your way, ready to pivot or change course. Experimenting and exploring also brings a little spice to life. If we wear something flashy, learn a new dance move, eat unique foods, or approach our partner with a fresh perspective, it can open new doors. Experimenting and exploring in little ways makes us ready for bigger considerations. Take the example of Taneesha.

Taneesha is a lively twenty-seven-year-old with a strong sense of herself and what she wants. She was raised to go for whatever she wanted by a proud and also-very-strong mother. She laughs at herself as she shares her experience.

> *A long time ago, I thought that if I wanted something badly enough and if I pictured it in my mind strong enough, I'd get it—just like I ordered. And sometimes I did! But then I began to notice that sometimes I didn't realize I'd gotten just exactly what I wanted, only it came in a different color, or shape or size, and I almost missed seeing it because I thought it should be in blue satin, size 8, instead. Maybe if I'd gotten the blue satin I wouldn't have been happy with it! I realized I had to be more flexible. It's kind of like putting in my order and trying it on to see if I like what I've ordered.*

Taneesha had learned this lesson in a big way when she was dating, and almost passed over, her husband, Lawrence.

> *I kept thinking I should be with Carl, a guy I was going out with for two years. I thought he had all the right qualifications—the ones that were on my wish list for a husband—and that we should get married. The only downside was, he was treating me badly. I had to be willing to see that what I really wanted was right around the corner in a different package than I thought I had ordered. Luckily, Lawrence was persistent enough to get me to experiment and see what I really wanted.*

Taneesha was not yet engaged to Carl and when Lawrence asked her out, she was open to reevaluating her choices. She was in an open-minded "experiment and explore" mode. She knew she could always change her mind. Lucky for her, she discovered all the qualities in Lawrence that she valued most highly.

> *He wasn't as tall, or as old, or as settled down, in a financial sense, as I thought I wanted, because I had a picture in my mind—maybe it was my mama's picture—of the man I was supposed to marry. Now that I'm a bit older, I'm sure I would be heading for divorce had I married that picture of a man.*

Taneesha had a big goal and a very specific idea of what she wanted in a man when she was in her early twenties, before she met Lawrence. But even when we're dealing with smaller goals and our minds are a bit more flexible, we may still need to experiment and explore—even though such experiments may not pan out the way we expect them to. Let's look at Maude and Paul's situation. As Paul explains it:

> *We both thought we wanted to live in the suburbs about ten years ago, when we had three little kids. Even though we were both raised in a medium-sized city.*

Says Maude:

Yeah, we should have found a way to check out suburban living without having to uproot ourselves and the kids, but I guess that was part of our experiment—to figure out where and how we all wanted to live.

Paul remarks:

It was a disruptive experiment, but now we all know. We sold our great old house and bought a big rambler about thirty-five minutes from downtown. We only lived there two years, because we just missed the city too much. We all had such strong ties to our old friends and neighbors, the city shops and cultural centers. We found ourselves constantly driving in to town!

Maude adds:

Finally, we just gave up and moved back to the city and into a different house in our old neighborhood. At least we know where we want to be, and everyone got the suburb fantasy out of their systems.

Then there is the example of Cal, who thought he wanted to become a painter when he was in his early thirties.

I was sure I wanted to do landscapes. I could see them in my mind and just needed to learn how to get them down on canvas. But I really had difficulty with the perspective and the small brushes. I'm a big guy with big hands that just got in the way of the fine details in my mind's eye. Luckily I had some patient and great teachers who encouraged me to try many different mediums. It took me a few years longer to experiment, but I learned so much. When I finally tried stone carving, the chisel and hammer fit right in my hands. The mass of the granite or marble or soapstone . . . mmmmm, they sing to me. I get lost in the chink chink, watching as the form emerges out of the stone. I love it.

Cal knows that he could have continued to try to paint and been far less satisfied. When he examined his core goal with his teachers, what was clear was that he wanted to make art. The medium became less important as he experimented. He let go of his original notion of making art and learned to enjoy the process of exploring. This exploration brought him the lodestone that is his current art and craft.

> *I never would have thought of carving huge chunks of stone on my own. Left to my own devices, I'd probably be an unhappy painter. It took the encouragement of others and a willingness to try new things to arrive at the profession that has satisfied my soul for well over thirty-five years.*

Then, following the examples of Taneesha, Maude and Paul, and Cal, this week, experiment and explore in two ways. First, try changing some of your little routines or habits to see how it feels, to spice things up, to get you out of ruts. Think about your goals and how rigidly you might hold to a specific vision of how you'd like things to turn out. Such a vision might lead to fulfillment, but it could also hinder you from seeing other possibilities—and prevent you from experimenting and exploring with your partner. Why not become more experimental and explore your goals together until you "feel your way" toward what is right for the two of you? You can still envision what you'd like, but, as you feel your way toward your goals, your choices become organic to both of you.

Let me further describe what I mean by choices evolving *organically*. It is the difference between following a goal created only in your head versus following a vision that satisfies both head and heart, a vision that develops with experience.

One reason change takes time is that we need time to learn from our experimentation—to sense whether we have become enriched by our experiences. I am not suggesting that you engage in experiments that cause you to stray from your goals. I am referring to the experiments and exploration that lead you to self-knowledge about what gives you pleasure, what suits you, what is truly satisfying. Sometimes it is like imagining that we want a big, juicy steak for dinner, only to find that it does not feel nourishing once you eat it. Maybe if you had explored the kitchen cupboards, you would have found that crackers and a bowl of soup would have satisfied your soul as well as your tummy. The steak is a vision; the soup becomes an organic choice upon exploration.

Sometimes experimentation and exploration open new doors, especially when you include other people's feedback, perspectives, thoughts, and experience. Not that you should follow their advice—but if you mix the ideas of others into your stew, sometimes it becomes tastier.

So, this week, your task is to stretch your creativity even further by consciously experimenting and exploring, individually and together.

EXERCISES

Experimenting and Exploring

Start by looking at one or two of your individual goals. Ask yourself, "Am I open to achieving this goal in many different forms, or do I have a rigid idea of what it must look like?" Write in your journal or workbook about this. Reflect on your experiences of goal setting. Think about whether you are like Taneesha, who almost passed over a good man because she had a rigid idea of what she wanted.

Next, make a list of all the ways you could experiment and explore as you work toward your goals in the coming weeks.

Now, come together and share what you discovered.

Then, as you work together on your partnership and family goals this week, come up with three or four ways you can experiment and explore—individually, together, as a family. What old assumptions about what you want should you question, and perhaps update or revise? How can you make your action steps more fun, playful, and creative? Whom might you consult for advice or feedback, together or individually?

Progress toward Your Individual Goals

As you continue to work toward your individual goals, review the following regularly:

- Your individual goal #1 (or #2, or #3).
- Your progress so far.
- The action steps you plan to take this week toward accomplishing this goal.
- Your potential for self-sabotage.

Each time you complete one of your goals, return to your main list of individual goals and choose the next goal you would like to work on. Set a date when you will decide on your action steps.

Progress toward Your Partnership Goals

Continue to work together on the action steps that will help you to accomplish the three partnership goals you identified in week 11, resolve difficult issues between you, and master daily details together. Remember that you are working to build a solid partnering foundation.

Once you have completed one of your partnership goals, choose another from the list you created in week 11 and begin to work on this goal together, so that you always have three goals—two less difficult and one more complex—to focus on at all times.

As you continue to work toward your goals together, review the following together at meetings:

- Your partnership goal #1 (or #2, or #3).
- Your progress so far.
- The action steps you plan to take this week toward accomplishing your goals.
- Your potential for self-sabotage, individually and together.
- Something special you plan to do this week as partners.

Progress toward Your Family Goal

Engage in the same process for your family goal this week. Involve the children in these discussions whenever appropriate. When you accomplish your current goal, choose another family goal from your one-year goal list that you created in week 11. At each family meeting, review the following:

- The family goal #1.
- Your progress so far as a family.
- The action steps you plan to take this week, individually and together, toward accomplishing your family goal.
- The potential for self-sabotage, both as a family and as individuals.
- Something special you will do as a family after the meeting.

Continuing Your Big Picture Adventure

Creating a master plan for living
the partnership of your dreams

You have worked together consistently and creatively these past weeks to strengthen your partnership. You have experienced the winning combination of the 10 Essentials plus your mutual creativity. Now you know you can create most of what you want at every age and stage of your lives.

This is the beginning of a life-long process. This week you will create a partnering datebook that will help you continue working toward your Big Picture goals—from the satisfying daily details to the juicy big dreams. Customize your datebook together as you continue to create the partnership, and life, of your dreams.

WHERE DO WE GO FROM HERE?

You may be asking the question, "Where do we go from here? We still have more goals on our one-year lists that we want to accomplish." You have daily details, maybe a few unresolved issues, and you may even be thinking about some future projects or dreams.

During the past fifteen weeks, you have spent time regularly talking and actively listening to one another. You have used all 10 Essentials and completed many exercises individually and then come together. You have written down your goals and taken action steps to accomplish them. This is the process you will continue. To do this you will:

- Regularly repeat the exercises in weeks 11 through 15 as you continue to balance your individual, partnership, and family goals and bring in new goals.

- Create a Big Picture datebook to reinforce the 10 Essentials and to continue working on your goals.

THE DATEBOOK

The aim of the datebook is to make the process continuous and ongoing throughout your lives. It is an agreement you make together to continue building your Big Picture.

The datebook will address both the daily details and your dreams. If you have not yet finished smoothing out the daily details or resolving unresolved issues, continue to make these your priority. Then, gradually, the Big Picture datebook can help you work toward those bigger goals and future dreams.

Perhaps your datebook will include future plans for how you want to live when the kids are grown and away from home. Maybe it will include a schedule of dialogue about where you want to go for that long-awaited vacation or sabbatical you have talked about for so long. Maybe you'll need to schedule talking times to discuss major career changes, starting a family, remodeling your home, or ways to play with your neighbors or contribute to your church or community. Whatever your vision might be, it is important to set new goals regularly in your life together. Your Big Picture partnering datebook will help you do so.

Here are some examples of how couples have used their partnering datebooks.

WILL YOUR DATEBOOK RESEMBLE REBA AND WARREN'S?

Reba and Warren are a couple in their late forties. They have no children and are both professionals with active careers. When Warren and Reba sat down to create their Big Picture datebook, they began by assessing how far they'd come since they began using the partnering approach. Warren recalled:

> There is no question, we are definitely committed to talking regularly —that is a given. It has improved our connection. Talking and making sure we do nice things for one another—both are a must! We've already become adept at getting these into our daily and weekly schedules.

Reba added:

> We're both happy with our connection, and we have completed work on three other household details that were problems before we got started.

Warren agreed:

> That's right. Our household routines—errands and grocery shopping, yard and auto upkeep, and taking turns cooking each night have gone

more smoothly. These used to be such a pain! We spent more time fighting about these things—and now, we just do them and spend time on our art projects or outdoor sports instead.

As they continued to share their experiences, Reba and Warren noted a few daily details that were still on their goal lists from week 16. One important area was financial planning. Warren said:

We've agreed to continue getting our finances under control in the next three to six months, especially as it will impact the long-range planning we want to do. We're agreeing to meet every other week for an hour to discuss action steps, look at the bills, consolidate our expenses, and plan ways to save money for the future.

Reba noted:

Our desire is to have completed our daily details goals six months from now so that those aspects of our lives are no-brainers. Then our goal is to look at what we like to create for fun in the coming ten-to-fifteen-years when we'll have more fun time and more free time.

Reba and Warren went on to describe the future goals they had established. Warren explained:

At this stage, we want to give back to the world. In evaluating our values and priorities, we got clear—we have no kids, we have enough money, and we still have lots of energy and half our lives left to live. We started to discuss and re-evaluate how to integrate giving something back to humanity. Our discussions are new and our brainstorming list includes everything from volunteering to build Habitat houses to joining the Red Cross Disaster Relief Teams, either nationally or internationally. Our goal is to come up with activities we can do each year that may eventually become our next "career" together.

Reba added:

Yeah—retirement as a career!

Warren noted a competing future goal they would need to face as they planned both finances and time:

Both of our parents are getting up there in age. So we are also preparing to care more for each of them as time goes on, and we're thinking about what that will require.

Reba and Warren then highlighted a list of topics to put in their datebook. Over the next few months, they would discuss one or two of these topics at each partnering meeting. As you'll note, most of these topics have to do with carving out more free time and balancing home and work. And then there's that one final item:

- Have a date night out, just the two of us, every other week
- Socialize with mutual friends, every other week
- Create more alone time
- Go to the health club three times a week (Reba)
- Run most mornings before work (Warren)
- Have dinner together most nights/coordinate so work meetings don't take precedence
- Attend monthly book club (Reba)
- Play squash or golf three to four times a month (Warren)
- Spice up our sex life!

Reba and Warren laughed as they were reminded of how much they still needed to keep balancing their daily details. Said Warren:

The difference now is that we don't take any of these needs for granted. We may not have figured out how to reach all of our goals yet, but we are committed to gradually reprioritizing how we spend our time.

Reba added:

Let's just say we are still in the brainstorming stage, until we come up with a few more options that we are ready to try. Since these are six-to-twelve month goals, we have a little time to rework how we do all of this together.

JOSH AND AMANDA'S DATEBOOK: A FAMILY AFFAIR

Josh and Amanda are in their mid-thirties with two children and a baby on the way. Erin is eight years old and Hannah is five. Here are Josh and Amanda's daily details goals which they'll list in their partnering datebook. Note how these issues highlight their stage in life and how their children are included in the scheduling.

- Stick to our regular talking times
- Figure out how Amanda can quit work and stay home once the baby comes
- Work together better as parents
- Keep practicing the Intentional Dialogue, so it becomes second nature and we don't have to schedule such long talks
- Put love-making on our future list—after the baby comes
- Continue our Sunday-afternoon family meetings
- Reevaluate how we want our parents involved once the baby arrives

And now listen in as Amanda and Josh discuss how they came up with their list. Amanda explains:

We're pretty good at talking, but it takes some effort to stick to our schedule. We both feel better when we stick to the regularly scheduled talking times. The girls notice the difference, too. We're more patient with each other and with them after we've had our talks—so they're calmer.

Also, we want to work harder on the basics, now, before the baby comes. Life will be more hectic in four months. In the past sixteen weeks we've made a lot of progress on communication skills, but they still need some work.

Josh added:

Amanda and I have a list of bigger things to keep working on, too—all are "in progress." A major issue is figuring out how Amanda can quit work and stay home once the baby comes. Our initial discussions were a major feat! They included working out the finances, my work-load, each of our ability to be with the kids, and so on. We celebrated after talking this through, that's for sure! I'm sure we will have to refine the plan when the baby is actually here.

Amanda continued:

Another area is working together better as parents. We thought we'd better get our parenting styles in sync before the third one comes along. Things were relatively smooth except around bedtime and getting the girls off to school and us out to work in the morning. We had to get some advice on how to get the youngest one to sleep in her own room—to give us some couple time—and to make her more secure. We have accomplished this during these sixteen weeks and everyone is feeling good. Hannah likes her new tape player and books that she can enjoy as she unwinds, and we have quiet time to do our talking, watch TV, *or cuddle.*

Josh added:

We also reviewed the basics of housekeeping, running the girls to their events, dinnertime at home more often, and less fast food for everyone. Other than the continuous pile of laundry and not getting the bathroom cleaned as often as I'd like, we both agreed we had these under control. On the other hand, we decided we need to keep practicing the Intentional Dialogue, so it becomes second nature.

Our communication got a lot better during these sixteen weeks, but we both know there are a few things under the surface that could erupt with the added pressure of a new baby. Amanda and I are feeling closer to each other since we began the Big Picture approach, and we want to prevent that distance between us from happening again. We agree to do one Intentional Dialogue a week for the next month, even if we have to hire a babysitter so that we can go sit in a coffee shop and have our talk.

And where does sexuality fit into Amanda and Josh's calendar? Amanda jokes:

Love-making, what's that? With this belly? Who has the time? Just kidding. It sounds nice, but right now with the pregnancy and the girls, it happens infrequently. We both enjoy it, but it is hard to find the time.

Josh agrees:

We definitely put that one on our future list. Maybe after the baby is a few months old and it will happen more naturally once we feel more skilled at the Intentional Dialogue we'll be able to talk about how to make it better. For now we decided to spend time cuddling for ten minutes at night and ten minutes in the morning, even if it's part of our regular talking time. And just to keep things sweet around here, we also reupped our commitment to remember lots of positives.

Josh and Amanda are also committed to including the girls in family meetings. Says Amanda:

We definitely need to continue those Sunday afternoon family meetings. We do it just before dinner and then try to have a fun dinner with family video time or a game right after. We talk about things we each like and need that week, and the girls really pitch in with their needs as well. They always like to vote on a video or activity. Ice cream and the kids' section at the bookstore are favorites.

Josh and I then plan our schedules in front of the girls, so everyone is included and they are aware of what's happening. They get to hear us plan our couple time, as well as our individual time with each of them. It helps them understand that we need time together, but we'll give them their special time, too.

Josh points out a discussion they need to have with their extended families before the baby arrives—and how a prediscussion with each other should be scheduled onto their Big Picture datebook.

Amanda and I have agreed to reevaluate how we want our parents involved once the baby arrives. We'll have to see what our needs are and talk to them about our decisions. So we scheduled a talking time in our datebook to discuss this with each other before we bring it up with our folks.

SUGGESTIONS FOR YOUR BIG PICTURE PARTNERING DATEBOOK TO MAINTAIN DAILY DETAILS AND BIG PICTURE VISIONS

Every relationship is different, and every couple has different needs and concerns. Throughout these past fifteen weeks, the Big Picture approach has enabled you to work together on your relationship by participating in a process you have customized according to your unique needs. I encourage you to similarly customize your Big Picture datebook using the following suggestions. You will know which things you need to emphasize and those you already do well.

Daily
- Maintain ongoing, respectful communication.
- Maintain positive feelings between you.
- Take time to appreciate one another and recognize your mutual resources.

During Each Week
- Schedule regular talking time every other day or four times a week; take turns talking and listening.
- Schedule social time together with others, depending on your needs that week.
- Schedule a weekly partnering meeting and/or family meeting followed by a fun activity or event.

Bi-Weekly and Monthly
- Schedule a partnering meeting to work on each goal established in week 11 (and each new goal that you establish). Incorporate dialogue to discuss big issues, plan a new project, or work toward future dreams. As you add new goals and create new action steps, keep track of your "to do" lists; report back on your accomplishments.

- Monthly Financial Meeting (to deal with finances—discuss bills, review financial needs and planning, maintain financial health).
- Schedule discussions of topics that you have agreed on, such as Warren and Reba's need to "give back to the world" when they retire, or Amanda and Josh's need to practice the Intentional Dialogue.

Every Three to Four Months
- Review your list of accomplishments and goals.
- Reevaluate and revise for the coming months.
- Celebrate your accomplishments!
- Review your daily details and goal-setting schedule. Delete those goals and action steps that have been completed and integrate new goals and action steps.

Every Six Months or Annually
- Revisit your commitment to one another and to partnering; acknowledge how far you have come.
- Reconsider your values and priorities; update them if necessary.
- Assess your short list of basic partnership needs and make sure you are addressing the ones that are relevant at the time. For example:

Household	Social
Financial	Sexual
Parenting	Spiritual
Work	Vacation, play
Intellectual pursuits	And others you agree on

- Introduce a longer-term goal and make it manageable by breaking it into smaller, doable action steps. Integrate these into your date-book for the coming months.

EXERCISES

Creating Your Big Picture Datebook

Because you have been doing the exercises each week and actively working toward your goals together, creating your Big Picture datebook should be quite simple.

Here are the steps:

Individually, each of you should review all the goals you set together in week 11, then review the progress you have made toward these goals in weeks 12 and 15.

Now, each of you should make three lists:

- Issues still unresolved
- Daily details not yet in progress
- Future goals you both have decided to work on within the year

Be sure to include everything on your individual, partnership, and family goal lists.

Note the things you have integrated and plan to continue, such as regularly talking and listening and keeping a positive feeling between you.

Next, still working individually, prioritize your goals from most important to least important in your life right now. Indicate which things you need to work on daily, weekly, monthly, every six months, and annually. Lastly, identify those things that involve your entire family.

Now, come together as partners as discuss your goals for the coming three to four months. Use mirroring and active listening to clarify what each of you desires.

Then make a master list of mutually agreed upon partnership and family goals, and individual goals that are appropriate at this time. Put everything that you are not able to work on during this time into a list for the future.

Once you have agreed upon the individual, partnership, and family goals you are going to work on in the coming three to four months, schedule conversations, dialogues, and meetings to accomplish your goals. Put these in your Big Picture datebook. As before, agree to be accountable and follow through.

CONTINUING YOUR BIG PICTURE JOURNEY

Creating a Master Plan for Living the Partnership of Your Dreams

Big Picture partnership is a journey, and your Big Picture datebook represents your map. Scheduling your regular touchstones together will help you to clearly envision and evaluate where you are headed. It will also keep you on track so that neither of you loses your bearings.

Once these practices and routines become second nature, you'll be a well-seasoned traveler who no longer needs a map. And you'll discover that you and your partner have the energy and time to enjoy each other to the fullest—and to create the ideal life you have envisioned together.

SOME FINAL WORDS OF ENCOURAGEMENT AND JOY

This is the point in most self-help books where authors wish their readers bon voyage, Godspeed, and good luck. Not me. That doesn't seem like enough.

You can't see me from where you are, so I want you to imagine me on the porch of my home, near a city lake. I'm laughing and smiling with delight as I prepare a toast.

Here's what I want the two of you to know:

I'm not going to wish you a polite, cursory bon voyage, because you're not just beginning your journey now. You and your partner started it long ago, when you first opened this book. And it's not some little journey across town. Sixteen weeks ago you took off on a bold, adventurous around-the-world cruise together. It's the trip of a life-time, and if you were to ever stop, you'd have all kinds of wonderful stories to tell one another.

Only you're not going to stop. Your journey together will last a lifetime, and if you keep practicing what you've learned here, you'll be living stories of wonder and awe and delight together month after month, year after year, and decade after decade.

I'm smiling because I'm filled with excitement for you. Because you're one of those rare couples that genuinely wants to achieve all the promise and joy that you are capable of bringing to each other. It makes me delighted to see the two of you committed to achieving great happiness and satisfaction together.

So, forget politeness and pallid good wishes. Here's my toast:

Dare to be great together, to fulfill your mission together, and to achieve your wildest dreams as a couple. Sail on together—each of you with one hand on the wheel, and one arm wrapped tightly around the other's waist.

If you look closely, you can see me on my porch, waving and cheering you on.

CHAPTER NOTES

WEEK 2

The 5-to-1 positive-to-negative ratio of interactions comes from the research of John Gottman, Ph.D. In various discussions of his findings, estimates predicting marital longevity range from 83–94%. See Sally MacDonald, "The State of Marriage in the 90s," *Seattle Times* (July 21, 1996); and John Mordecai Gottman, Ph.D. and Robert Wayne Levenson, Ph.D., "Rebound from Marital Conflict and Divorce Population," *Family Process,* vol. 38, no. 3 (1999): pp 287–292. Dr. Gottman has published many books on his research that are useful for marriage educators and couples, all of which are recommended to the reader. Among them is the popular *Why Marriages Succeed or Fail and How You Can Make Yours Last,* by John M. Gottman, Ph.D., and Nan Silver, Fireside: New York, 1995.

WEEK 3

Various information from 2000 Census statistics and Smart Marriage press release, July 2001, "What's all the commotion?" indicate that approximately 86% of all people in the United States are married at least once in their lifetime.

The characteristics of happy healthy adults are drawn from the author's clinical experience as well as research and clinical resources. For further information on healthy adult development the author recommends the reader to Erik Erickson's social theory of psychology, Abraham Maslow's hierarchy of needs, and any of the following authors and the full range of their book titles. Included here are just a few.

Seligman, Martin E., Ph.D. *Authentic Happiness: Using New Positive Psychology to Realize Your Potential for Lasting Fulfillment.* Free Press: New York, 2002.

Vaillant, George E. *Aging Well: Surprising Guideposts to a Happier Life from the Landmark Harvard Study of Adult Development.* Little, Brown: New York, 2003.

Sheehy, Gail. *New Passages: Mapping Your Life Across Time.* Random House: New York, 1995.

Sheehy, Gail. *Understanding Men's Passages: Discovering the New Map of Men's Lives.* Ballantine: New York, 1999.

Goleman, Daniel. *Emotional Intelligence: Why it Can Matter More than IQ.* Bantam: New York, 1997.

I also refer to the early work of Sandra Bem, Ph.D., currently professor of psychology and women's studies at Cornell University, and her studies of masculine and feminine characteristics and how they impact self-esteem, as studied with a Sex Role Inventory. When queried via email, Dr. Bem could not recall the specific article I was referring to, however, you may find any of her articles interesting, as well as the following book: Sandra Bem, Ph.D. *The Lenses of Gender: Transforming the Debate on Sexual Inequality.* Yale University Press: Cambridge, MA, 1994.

The parent/adult/child model comes out of Transactional Analysis (TA) which is a social psychology developed by Eric Berne, M.D. Over the past forty years the theory has been adopted for use in many fields including psychotherapy, counseling, education, and organizational development. A major text from TA is *I'm OK–You're OK,* by Thomas Harris, Ph.D. Reissued by Avon: New York, 1993.

WEEK 5

A wide variety of resources cite divorce for marrieds and break-up of those who co-habit around 50% for marrieds and higher for those who co-habit. Some of this is found in documentation from the Rutgers' National Marriage Project, Census Bureau statistics, articles and communications with Mike McManus of Marriage Savers, www.marriagesavers.com and Dr. Neil Warren.

From unpublished research by Linda J. Waite, as found in *The Top Ten Myths of Divorce* by David Popenoe, Director of The National Marriage Project, 86% of people who were unhappily married in the late 1980s and stayed with the marriage, indicated when interviewed five years later that they were happier.

A classic discussion of long-term love and commitment is found in M. Scott Peck's book *The Road Less Traveled, 25th Anniversary Edition: A New Psychology of Love, Traditional Values and Spiritual Growth.* Touchstone: New York, 2003.

Another useful resource for couples and clients is a small and inexpensive pamphlet entitled, "Intimacy," by Marilyn Mason, Ph.D., L.C.P., Hazelden: Center City, MN, 1986.

WEEK 7

The concept of 100% involvement on the part of each partner, and win/win solutions is drawn from the work of Gay and Kathlyn Hendricks, especially their early work, *Conscious Loving: The Journey to Co-Commitment.* Bantam: New York, 1992.

The intentional dialogue is taken directly from the work of Harville Hendrix. Various versions of the dialogue process can be found online at a number of Imago Therapy websites, however the version utilized in this book is a translation, from the author's experience in a workshop with Harville Hendrix himself. Dr. Hendrix's best known work is *Getting the Love You Want: A Guide For Couples.* Owl Books: New York, 2001.

The quote from Marianne Williamson can be found in *A Return to Love, Reflections on the Principles of a Course in Miracles,* Harper Collins: New York, 1992. www.Marianne.com

Citations of various programs that teach negotiation and communication skills include The Program on Negotiation at Harvard University's Law School and The Brave New Workshop Theatre in Minneapolis Minnesota. Books related to the Harvard program include:

Fisher, Roger, and Scott Brown. *Getting Together: Building Relationships as We Negotiate.* Penguin: New York, 1989.

Fisher, Roger, Bruce Patten, and William Ury. *Getting to Yes: Negotiating Agreement Without Giving In.* 2nd ed. Penguin: New York, 1991.

The Brave New Workshop Theatre in Minneapolis, Minnesota, was founded by Dudley Riggs in 1958. In their improvisational training sessions for corporate audiences they blend education and entertainment into a fun, unique, "hands-on" experience in a safe, creative environment that participants help to create. www.bravenewworkshop.com

WEEK 9

The full reference for Eileen McCann's book, enthusiastically mentioned in this chapter is: McCann, Eileen. *The Two-Step: The Dance Toward Intimacy.* Grove Press: New York, 1987.

Research on relationship longevity discussed in week 2, as well as the ability to resolve conflicts, again comes from John Gottman, Ph.D. Dr. Gottman also endorses calming methods when a couple is in the midst of a conflict. He refers to this as "gentle de-escalation and soothing," that are better than active listening techniques or mirroring when a couple is in the midst of a conflict. This specific sources comes from a 1999 *Futurist* article entitled "Predicting Successful Marriages," (Cynthia G. Wagner, vol. 33, no. 6, June/July 1999), received from Dr. Gottman's office.

Additional studies and clinical applications on the topic of conflict resolution include work by Clifford Notarius, Scott Stanley, and Howard Markman. Some additional titles include:

Markman, Howard, Scott Stanley, and Susan L. Blumberg. *Fighting for Your Marriage: Positive Steps for Preventing Divorce and Preserving a Lasting Love.* Jossey-Bass: San Francisco, 2001.

Notarius, Clifford, Clifford Notarius I., and Howard Markman, ed. *We Can Work It Out: How to Solve Conflicts, Save Your Marriage, and Strengthen Your Love for Each Other.* Perigee: New York, 1994.

Drs. John and Julie Gottman conduct couples workshops throughout the year in Seattle, Washington. During the workshop, couples gain new insights and learn research-based relationship skills that can improve the intimacy and friendship in their relationship. More information can be found at their website www.gottman.com.

One of the most successful programs for couples in trouble is PREP: The Prevention and Relationship Enhancement Program, founded and directed by Howard Markman, Ph.D. and

Scott Stanley, Ph.D. PREP is based on over twenty years of research and can be found online at www.prepinc.com.

WEEKS 11—15

There are a wide variety of creativity resources available on the bookshelves and online. For initial grounding in this topic, the author highly recommends the following resources:

Bepko, Claudia, and Jo-Ann Krestan. *Singing at the Top of Our Lungs: Women, Love, and Creativity.* HarperCollins: New York, 1993.

Cameron, Julia. *The Artist's Way: A Spiritual Path to Higher Creativity.* Putnam: New York, 1992.

Czikszentmihalyi, Mihaly. *Creativity: Flow and the Psychology of Discovery and Invention.* HarperCollins: New York, 1997.

Czikszentmihalyi, Mihaly. *Flow: The Psychology of Optimal Experience.* HarperCollins: New York, 1990.

Fritz, Robert. *Creating.* Ballantine: New York, 1993.

Fritz, Robert. *The Path of Least Resistance: Learning to Become the Creative Force in Your Own Life.* Revised and expanded. Fawcett Columbine: New York, 1989.

Harman, Willis, Ph.D., and Howard Rheingold. *Higher Creativity: Liberating the Unconscious for Breakthrough Insights.* Tarcher: New York, 1984.

RESOURCES

Smart Marriages

One of the main resources for both couples and marriage education professionals is The Coalition for Marriage, Couples, and Family Education, LLC. This comprehensive and free service, founded and run by Diane Sollee, M.S.W., can be viewed online at www.smartmarriages.com.

Smart Marriages exists for the betterment and promotion of research, education, legislation, and support of healthy relationships. You can receive an informative online newsletter, use the extensive directory to look up a class or workshop anywhere in the world, and become connected to the very latest research, books, and resources available through this resource.

Smart Marriages also provides an annual conference each summer where upwards of 2500 people gather from all over the nation, and the world, to discuss, promote, become informed about, and celebrate healthy marriage. This low-cost, annual event provides great opportunity to network with other couples, marriage educators, peer mentors, and a wide variety of other experts in an informal atmosphere. The format involves pre and post training Institutes for couples and educators, a wide variety of exhibitors, lunch and dinner presentations by leaders in the field, and a large number of informative workshops throughout the entire three-day conference itself.

The National Marriage Project

This initiative, located at Rutgers University, is co-directed by two leading family experts and well-known authors, David Popenoe, Ph.D., and Barbara Dafoe Whitehead, Ph.D. Its mission is to strengthen the institution of marriage by providing research that informs public policy, educates the public, and focuses attention on the consequences of problems in marriage on the millions of children in our nation.

The National Marriage Project website can be viewed online at www.marriage.rutgers.edu. It includes a list of publications and links that are informative and useful.

INDEX

say yes, 159–161
talk with your partner, 93–96
explore and experiment, 267–275
express appreciation, 164–166

F

family goals, 239, 249, 255–256, 266, 274–275
family values and priorities, 127–129
family visits and partnering skills, 131–132
fight-or-flight response to conflict, 198–199
formal commitment, 106–107

G

goals of the heart, 227–239
Gottman, John M., 35–36, 193

H

handle emotions, 71–74
healthy adults and maturity, 65–66

I

Imago Therapy, 209
impeccable behavior, 149
individual concerns as partnership concerns, 159–161
individual goals, 234–235, 247–248, 254–255, 265, 273–274
individual resources, 167
Intentional Dialogue, 207–226
intimate relationships, 54

L

life purpose, 54
look back in awe, 163–172

M

masculine and feminine aspects of selves, 52
master plan, 277–289
meaningful connections between partners, 25–26
Merged partnering, 8–12
mirroring: Intentional Dialogue, 214–217, 220
mutual appreciation, 167–169
mutual creativity, 27–28
mutual options, 258–263

N

navigate change, 100–104
negative interactions: taking each other for granted, 39–41
nurture yourselves, 47–81

O

one day at a time, 115–116
our world decisions, 22–24, 142–147
outside support for partnership, 130–133

P

Parent/Adult/Child selves, 56, 57, 67
Parent self, 56–60, 58, 59
Critical Parent, 59–60
partnering agreements, 150–152
partnering styles, 3–32
partners as teammates, 153–156
partnership as priority, 121–140
partnership (mutual) goals, 235–237, 246–247, 248, 255, 265–266, 274
personal responsibility for relationship, 147–149
please your partner, 42–44
positive interactions, 33–46
priorities and values, 134–140

ACKNOWLEDGMENTS

Writing a book can be a very lonely process, but for me it has been exhilarating to experience the community that has encircled this project and believed in its message. The natural evolution of this community and the many partnerships that have developed speak volumes about the human urge to create great relationships and the desire to share this knowledge with others.

First, I would like to gratefully acknowledge my primary mentors: the many clients I have worked with over the years. I am always humbled by their tenacity, perseverance, and desire to make their lives and relationships more meaningful, as well as their courage and vulnerability in opening up to me. They have been my greatest teachers. I thank them for the daily challenge to see what is unique in each situation and to continuously become more creative.

From the beginning, longtime friend and colleague Robert Baker was ever-ready with tools that helped me get out of my own way and let my muse speak more freely.

Book designer Dorie McClelland believed in both the project and me, even when I floundered. Then she worked her magic on the pages.

Research assistance by Marcia Jedd was invaluable.

My editors and my writing and marketing consultants have been worth their weight in gold. They have also been enormously kind. I have learned much from each of them about the art of connecting with my readers. Paulette Bates-Alden patiently edited the first draft and insightfully helped shape the book. Laura Westlund offered valuable editorial input, and media savant Martin Keller provided a marketing perspective. Laila Schirrmeister generously contributed to the stories. Alice Erickson and Kara Pederson gave time and careful attention to details. Writer and book editor Laura Golden Bellotti edited the final manuscript, meeting every deadline and making my words reader-friendly. And throughout the final drafts, writing consultant Scott Edelstein enthusiastically went toe-to-toe with key concepts and language, helping to clarify and match the book's tone with my intent.

Cover designer Deb Miner then did the same with her unique visuals, blending beauty with playfulness.

And then there is Megan Hollon, Twofold Publication's Publicity Director and Jill-of-All-Trades. You have been a delight. Together we move mountains in the world of book promotion in no time at all. I am grateful you are on my team.

Many others have sustained me as I brought this book to life. I have been befriended, cheered on, fed well, entertained, counseled wisely, and accompanied on travels. My home has been cleaned; my computer has been upgraded and kept in good running order; my body and voice have been kept in tune; my dog Tara has never missed a walk, and my cats Chloe and Nipper have been consistently well cared for. Family, old friends, new friends, and neighbors have cared for me well and in many ways. Your care and friendship have meant much to me.

BIG PICTURE PARTNERING

WORKSHOPS, RETREATS, AND COACHING

for Couples, Peer Mentors, and Professionals

Dr. Jan Hoistad routinely offers a variety of ways to help you get the Big Picture, through classes, workshops, retreats, and personal consultations. All are designed to give you ample time and skills for learning, dreaming, and growing together. Go on-line, call, or email to determine which option is best for you.

WORKSHOPS:

Workshops are regularly scheduled in these centrally-located cities: Minneapolis, Vancouver, and the Carolinas.
Log on to the website for a complete, up-to-date calendar.

TELE-WORKSHOPS:

Designed as a unique way for couples at a distance to work together over a 16 week period, tele-workshops start at a centrally-located retreat followed by monthly tele-conferenced group sessions with Dr. Jan. Check out this option online.

PERSONALIZED CONSULTATIONS:

Personalized individual or couples coaching directly with Dr. Jan—in person, via email, or phone—may be just the right option for you.

RESOURCES AND TRAINING FOR PROFESSIONALS AND PEER MENTORS:

Go online for our latest books and resources, including out-of-the-box training kits, workshops, and CEU options.

For more information, or to book Dr. Jan for a workshop in your area:

Call toll free **1.888.231.2993**

Email: **info@bigpicturepartnering.com**

www.bigpicturepartnering.com

BIG PICTURE PARTNERING

CURRENT PRODUCTS

Order Big Picture Products Online

BOOKS AND WORKBOOKS:

Big Picture Partnering: 16 weeks to a rock-solid relationship, and
Big Picture Partnering Workbook, a stand-alone or companion exercise guide.

BIG PICTURE PARTNERING SUPPLIES:

Couples, peer mentors, and professionals, will find these additional supplies
helpful for personal and group use.

Packets of: 10 Essentials
                Time-Outs
                How to Dialogue
                Big Picture Notepads
                Big Picture Post-Its

AVAILABLE SOON

Look for Big Picture Audio/Video Training tapes for couples and professionals, along with other new products:

www.bigpicturepartnering.com